P9-CQD-753

NEW DIRECTIONS FOR TEACHING AND LEARNING

Robert J. Menges, *Northwestern University*
EDITOR-IN-CHIEF

Marilla D. Svinicki, *University of Texas, Austin*
ASSOCIATE EDITOR

Bringing Problem-Based Learning to Higher Education: Theory and Practice

LuAnn Wilkerson
University of California, Los Angeles

Wim H. Gijselaers
University of Limburg, Maastricht, the Netherlands

EDITORS

Number 68, Winter 1996

JOSSEY-BASS PUBLISHERS
San Francisco

BRINGING PROBLEM-BASED LEARNING TO HIGHER EDUCATION:
THEORY AND PRACTICE
LuAnn Wilkerson, Wim H. Gijselaers (eds.)
New Directions for Teaching and Learning, no. 68
Robert J. Menges, Editor-in-Chief
Marilla D. Svinicki, Associate Editor

Microfilm copies of issues and articles are available in 16mm and 35mm, as well as microfiche in 105mm, through University Microfilms Inc., 300 North Zeeb Road, Ann Arbor, Michigan 48106-1346.

ISSN 0271-0633   ISBN 0-7879-9934-2

NEW DIRECTIONS FOR TEACHING AND LEARNING is part of The Jossey-Bass Higher and Adult Education Series and is published quarterly by Jossey-Bass Inc., Publishers, 350 Sansome Street, San Francisco, California 94104-1342. Periodicals postage paid at San Francisco, California, and at additional mailing offices. POSTMASTER: Send address changes to New Directions for Teaching and Learning, Jossey-Bass Inc., Publishers, 350 Sansome Street, San Francisco, California 94104-1342.

SUBSCRIPTIONS cost $52.00 for individuals and $79.00 for institutions, agencies, and libraries.

EDITORIAL CORRESPONDENCE should be sent to the editor-in-chief, Robert J. Menges, Northwestern University, Center for the Teaching Professions, 2115 North Campus Drive, Evanston, Illinois 60208-2610.

Cover photograph by Richard Blair/Color & Light © 1990.

Manufactured in the United States of America on Lyons Falls Pathfinder Tradebook. This paper is acid-free and 100 percent totally chlorine-free.

CONTENTS

98089

FROM THE SERIES EDITORS

About This Publication. Since 1980, *New Directions for Teaching and Learning (NDTL)* has brought a unique blend of theory, research, and practice to leaders in postsecondary education. *NDTL* sourcebooks strive not only for solid substance but also for timeliness, compactness, and accessibility.

The series has four goals: to inform readers about current and future directions in teaching and learning in postsecondary education, to illuminate the context that shapes these new directions, to illustrate these new directions through examples from real settings, and to propose ways in which these new directions can be incorporated into still other settings.

This publication reflects our view that teaching deserves respect as a high form of scholarship. We believe that significant scholarship is conducted not only by researchers who report results of empirical investigations but also by practitioners who share disciplined reflections about teaching. Contributors to *NDTL* approach questions of teaching and learning as seriously as they approach substantive questions in their own disciplines, and they deal not only with pedagogical issues but also with the intellectual and social context in which these issues arise. Authors deal on the one hand with theory and research and on the other with practice, and they translate from research and theory to practice and back again.

About This Volume. Problem-based learning promises much in helping students learn to think. This volume describes the growth of PBL from early days in medical schools to current uses in a variety of fields. The authors make a persuasive argument that professional fields as well as academic fields would find much to recommend PBL as a standard teaching method.

Robert J. Menges, *Editor-in-Chief*
Marilla D. Svinicki, *Associate Editor*

EDITORS' NOTES

> Problem-based learning is the learning that results from the process
> of working toward the understanding or resolution of a problem.
> The problem is encountered first in the learning process.
> —Barrows and Tamblyn, 1980, p. 2

In the 1960s and 1970s, a group of medical educators became increasingly aware of the need to rethink how and what to teach to better prepare physicians for the demands of professional practice (Barrows and Tamblyn, 1980). They criticized traditional health sciences education for its excessive emphasis on memorization, its fragmentation, and its failure to equip graduates with the problem-solving skills required for a lifetime of learning. They argued that professional practice required skills in problem solving, including an ability to acquire essential data, to synthesize that data into possible hypotheses, and to test those hypotheses through the acquisition of additional data, a process they called hypothetico-deductive reasoning.

It was this particular issue that led faculty members at McMaster University to develop a problem-based curriculum for their new medical school. Traditional basic science and clinical disciplines were approached from a multidisciplinary perspective. Problems were used as a stimulus for learning. Students worked in small groups led by a faculty member referred to as a *tutor,* whose role it was to facilitate learning by asking questions and monitoring the problem-solving processes. Over the past thirty years, problem-based learning has been adopted by medical schools all around the world. More recently, it has been applied in a variety of other professional schools (Gijselaers and others, 1995). Now interest is increasing throughout higher education in this and other interactive forms of education.

The present volume addresses problem-based learning from the perspective of theory and practice. The first three chapters explore the links between theory, research, and practice in problem-based learning. In the next seven chapters, faculty members describe how they have applied problem-based learning in their various disciplines, including business education, biology, chemistry, physics, educational leadership, general education, architecture, and calculus. Drawing on their own experience, they offer suggestions for planning, designing, and implementing problem-based courses. We think that you will find two common themes particularly interesting: the variety of classroom arrangements used in implementing problem-based learning in college courses and the types of problems developed. We hope that the collection will stimulate you to design or redesign problem-based learning practices in your own courses so as to effectively engage students in developing both a context-rich knowledge base and a set of skills in applying that knowledge to the under-standing and resolution of meaningful problems throughout a lifetime of learning.

LuAnn Wilkerson
Wim H. Gijselaers
Editors

References

Barrows, H. S., and Tamblyn, R. N. *Problem-Based Learning: An Approach to Medical Education*. New York: Springer, 1980.

Gijselaers, W. H., Tempelaar, D. T., Keizer, P. K., Blommaert, J. M., Bernard, E. M., and Kasper, H. (eds.). *Educational Innovation in Economics and Business Administration: The Case of Problem-Based Learning*. Norwell, Mass.: Kluwer, 1995.

LUANN WILKERSON is associate dean for medical education and director of the Center for Educational Development and Research, University of California, Los Angeles, School of Medicine.

WIM H. GIJSELAERS is associate professor of education at the department of educational development and educational research, University of Limburg, Maastricht, the Netherlands.

This chapter reviews the motivation for the change to problem-based learning, its definition, and the educational objectives it can serve. It discusses changing an established curriculum to problem-based learning and asks whether problem-based learning is worth the trouble.

Problem-Based Learning in Medicine and Beyond: A Brief Overview

Howard S. Barrows

Designing a new curriculum, developing new teaching tools, training faculty to develop new teaching skills, and nurturing students through a fundamental change in learning is an expensive and time-consuming effort. Twenty-five years ago, a newly created medical school went to this trouble, and in the ensuing years, many others have followed suit.

A brief review of the factors that motivated the need for curricular change will serve as an introduction to problem-based learning (PBL). The McMaster University Faculty of Health Sciences established a new medical school with an innovative educational approach to be used throughout its entire three-year curriculum, an approach now known the world around as problem-based learning. It graduated its first class in 1972. At about the same time, the College of Human Medicine at Michigan State University implemented a problem-solving course as a separate track in its preclinical curriculum (Jones and others, 1984). Stimulated by the McMaster approach, and with cross-fertilization, other newly created medical schools in Maastricht (the Netherlands) and in Newcastle (Australia) also developed problem-based learning curricula in the early 1970s. By the early 1980s, medical schools with conventional curricula began to develop alternative, parallel problem-based curricula for a subset of their students. The leader in this trend was the Primary Care Curriculum at the University of New Mexico. Later on, other schools took on an even more arduous task of converting their entire curriculum to problem-based learning. The leader was the University of Hawaii, followed by Harvard (which had first established an alternative track) and the University of Sherbrooke in Canada.

New Directions for Teaching and Learning, no. 68, Winter 1996 © Jossey-Bass Publishers

Now there are new and established medical schools all around the globe that have developed or are developing problem-based curricula. What was the motivation behind all this effort?

In 1969, just as McMaster was getting under way, Spaulding (1969) described the motivation for creating an innovative approach: "Current dissatisfaction with medical education imposes on a new medical school a responsibility of experimenting with novel approaches" (p. 659). The McMaster group noted that students were disenchanted and bored with their medical education because they were saturated by the vast amounts of information they had to absorb, much of which was perceived to have little relevance to medical practice. They also noted that, by contrast, during residency, students were excited by working with patients and solving problems (Spaulding, 1991, p. 28).

In describing the innovative problem-based track at Michigan State, Jones and others (1984) stated that during curriculum planning it was "accepted that education in the techniques of medical problem-solving should be a part of the College's preclerkship curriculum" (pp. 181–182). My own motivation for developing a specific problem-based learning approach was similar. Studies of the clinical reasoning of students and resident physicians in neurology suggested that the conventional methods of teaching probably inhibit, if not destroy, any clinical reasoning ability (Barrows and Bennett, 1972). This, together with the observation that students had forgotten their freshman neuroanatomy by the time of their clinical neurology course as juniors, an observation reinforced by the studies of Levine and Forman (1973), led to my design of a method stressing development of the clinical reasoning or problem-solving process for the neuroscience unit of the McMaster curriculum (Barrows, 1984). This approach has been further developed in the alternative curriculum at Southern Illinois University (Barrows, 1994).

A wider dissemination of problem-based learning in the United States resulted from the *Report of the Panel on the General Professional Education of the Physician and College Preparation for Medicine,* known as the "GPEP report" (Muller, 1984) sponsored by the Association of American Medical Colleges. This report made many recommendations for changes in medical education, such as promoting independent learning and problem solving, reducing lecture hours, reducing scheduled time, and evaluating the ability to learn independently. These were perceived as support for problem-based learning by many medical school deans and faculty who were, as a consequence of this report, initiating curricular reviews.

Now countless medical schools in the United States have developed or are developing problem-based curricula in courses, alternative curricula, or as an entire curriculum revision. Many schools, particularly those with long traditions, want to create their own variation of problem-based learning that reflects their rigor and excellence. This often includes blending problem-based learning with elements of their conventional teaching into a hybrid, as a compromise with faculty unconvinced about the value of problem-based learning. All these approaches to problem-based learning represent such a wide variety of methods that now the term has far less precision than might be assumed (Barrows, 1986).

The Definition of Problem-Based Learning

In spite of the many variations of PBL that have evolved during its dissemination as a new method in medical education, a core model or basic definition with which others can be compared is needed. The original method developed at McMaster works well as this model. Its characteristics are these.

Learning Is Student-Centered. Under the guidance of a tutor (as described later in this chapter), the students must take responsibility for their own learning, identifying what they need to know to better understand and manage the problem on which they are working and determining where they will get that information (books, journals, faculty, on-line information resources, and so forth). "Resource faculty" in many different subject areas are available to the students as consultants. This allows each student to personalize learning so as to concentrate on areas of limited knowledge or understanding, and to pursue areas of interest.

Learning Occurs in Small Student Groups. In most of the early PBL medical schools, groups were made up of five to eight or nine students. Characteristically, at the end of each curricular unit, the students are resorted randomly into new groups with a new tutor. This gives them practice in working intensely and effectively with a variety of different people.

Teachers Are Facilitators or Guides. At McMaster the group facilitator was referred to as a *tutor.* This role was often defined in negative terms. It was someone who did not give students a lecture or factual information, did not tell the students whether they were right or wrong in their thinking, and did not tell them what they ought to study or read. The role is better understood in terms of metacognitive communication. The tutor asks students the kinds of questions that they should be asking themselves to better understand and manage the problem (Barrows, 1988). Eventually the students take on this role themselves, challenging each other. To inhibit the tutor from falling back on old teaching reflexes and giving the students direct information and guidance, McMaster promoted the concept of the "non-expert" tutor. This meant that tutors should perform in curricular units where they were not content experts. It seems generally agreed now that the best tutors are those who are expert in the area of study, only they must also be expert in the difficult role of tutor.

Problems Form the Organizing Focus and Stimulus for Learning. In PBL for medicine, a patient problem or a community health problem is presented in some format, such as a written case, case vignette, standardized (also called *simulated*) patient, computer simulation, videotape. It represents the challenge students will face in practice and provides the relevance and motivation for learning. In attempting to understand the problem, students realize what they will need to learn from the basic sciences. The problem thus gives them a focus for integrating information from many disciplines. The new information is also associated with cues patient problems present. All this facilitates later recall and application to future patient problems.

Problems Are a Vehicle for the Development of Clinical Problem-Solving Skills. For this to happen, the problem format has to present the patient problem in the same way that it occurs in the real world, with only the patient's presenting complaints or symptoms. The format should also permit the students to ask the patient questions, carry out physical examinations, and order laboratory tests, all in any sequence. The students should get the results of these inquiries as they work their way through the problem. Such formats as the "P4" (Barrows and Tamblyn, 1977), the Problem-Based Learning Module (Distlehorst and Barrows, 1982), standardized patients (Barrows, 1987), and computer simulations can allow for free inquiry as in clinical practice.

New Information Is Acquired Through Self-Directed Learning. As a corollary to the characteristics already described (the student-centered curriculum and the teacher as facilitator of learning), the students are expected to learn from the world's knowledge and accumulated expertise by virtue of their own study and research, just as real practitioners do. During this self-directed learning, students work together, discussing, comparing, reviewing, and debating what they have learned.

Educational Objectives Possible with a Problem-Based Curriculum

These were the original characteristics for problem-based learning before its dissemination in medicine and elsewhere. This model makes the educational objectives listed in this section possible. Each objective is followed by a description of curricular design elements needed to address the objective.

The Acquisition of an Integrated Knowledge Base. For this to happen, all medical school disciplines basic to medical practice need to be incorporated into the problem-based learning curriculum. In a number of schools, some disciplines are taught outside the problem-based learning curriculum. Not only does this inhibit integration of those subjects in the students' understanding of a patient's problem, it also requires students to move in and out of different learning approaches, passive versus active, dependent versus independent. Many disciplines beyond the usual basic sciences, such as behavior, humanities, community health, ethics, epidemiology, need to be incorporated into the curriculum.

The Acquisition of a Knowledge Base Structured Around the Cues Presented by Patient Problems. By organizing their knowledge around patient cues, medical students enhance their ability to recall what they have learned and apply it in clinical work. This objective could be accomplished by any problem-based learning curriculum in which students analyze and resolve the problem as far as possible before acquiring any information needed for better understanding. This objective may represent the absolutely irreducible core of problem-based learning, if such a thing were to be articulated.

The Acquisition of a Knowledge Base Enmeshed with Problem-Solving Processes Used in Clinical Medicine. The Development of an Effective and Efficient Clinical Problem-Solving Process. These two objectives cannot be realized unless patient problems are presented in a format that allows students to use the problem-solving skills needed in practice. For example, the problem-based curriculum at Southern Illinois University stresses the use of patient formats such as the PBLM (Distlehorst and Barrows, 1982) and standardized patients to allow students to inquire freely of the patient. By contrast, the problem-based curriculum at Maastricht presents students with patient problem protocols that contain most of the information needed to analyze and resolve the problem. The faculty feel it is inappropriate for undergraduate students to be in the vocational context of being a physician while they are in the academic pursuit of knowledge basic to medicine. These cognitive skills would be developed in their later clinical work (W. H. Gijselaers, personal communication, 1994). Other schools use formats that only develop some skills in problem solving (Barrows, 1990). This point is not appreciated by those making the observation that problem-based learning students do not seem to have better problem-solving skills when compared to students in conventional curricula (Barrows, 1996). In many problem-based learning curricula, the development of these skills is not addressed.

The Development of Effective Self-Directed Learning Skills. The Development of Team Skills. These goals require that the PBL approach be student-centered. Students must be able to determine on their own what to learn and from what resources, guided by the facilitator or tutor. This educational goal is easily weakened by tutors who are directive with students, by faculty statements about learning expectations with each problem, by reading assignments paired with problems, by resource faculty who tell the students what they should know as opposed to answering their questions, and by faculty-generated multiple choice questions to assess student progress. All these tend to make the students dependent on the faculty telling them what to learn, as in conventional curricula, instead of being the independent learners that they must be in medical practice.

There are other educational goals that could be added. There are also many other variables that can confound these goals, such as the expected role of the tutor, the tutor training employed, the size of the student group, and the existence of competing curricular activities outside of PBL.

If effort, money, and time are to be invested in developing a PBL curriculum, it would seem worthwhile to achieve all the possible advantages of the method. Compromises are often made by schools or teachers unaware of all that PBL can accomplish and of the damage that apparently easy or trivial compromises in curricular design can do to this potential.

Changing an Established Curriculum to Problem-Based Learning

Most medical schools that have changed to problem-based learning share several characteristics. The dean either encourages PBL or provides visible support to a faculty group that wants to change to PBL. There is also a group of internally credible faculty members from both the clinical and basic sciences who want to change to PBL and are willing to spend the time and effort necessary.

Other factors that contribute to curricular change are visits by both enthusiastic and skeptical faculty members to schools using PBL and a demonstration of PBL at the school, using the school's own students. It also helps to have interested faculty members go through a PBL experience themselves to appreciate the motivation and desire to learn that is produced despite their already established expertise in medicine. Presentations and lectures about problem-based learning are unconvincing—the listeners conjure up their own ideas as to what the method is like based on their own past experiences. Demonstration and experience make all the difference. If problem-based learning is to be tried, it should be given the opportunity to flourish.

The Curriculum in Problem-Based Learning

The previously stated goals for PBL describe skills that can be developed with this method—problem-solving, self-directed learning, and team or collaborative learning skills. They also suggest that the nature of learning is active, integrated, and associated with the cues present in real-world professional problems (patients) and the cognitive processes used in problem solving. They do not circumscribe the subject matter of the curriculum. An outsider cannot review these goals and determine what the students will learn in a problem-based curriculum. In fact, as the method is student-centered and self-directed, an outsider might mistakenly assume that PBL is chaos or a free educational happening with students learning whatever they wish. The curricular linchpin in PBL—the thing that holds it together and keeps it on track—is the collection of problems in any given course or curriculum with each problem designed to stimulate student learning in areas relevant to the curriculum.

In some PBL curricula, the areas of expected learning with each problem (so-called learning objectives) are written down. This list is not made available to the students until after they have carried out all the self-directed learning they feel is needed and have finished their work with the problem. The list serves as a guide to faculty tutors not expert in the subject under study. It helps them guide students into areas of discussion that lead to productive learning. The objectives can also be assembled into a matrix with the problem titles across the top and the expected content objectives for the course listed down the side. Under each problem title, the subject matter addressed (in the mind of the course director) is checked off. There usually is redundancy as several problems may address similar areas of content, but that is all to the good. This matrix allows course directors and anyone else interested to see the putative course content. A major advantage of PBL is that the students, responsible for their own learning and engaged in self-directed learning and stimulated by the problem, may pursue areas of study far beyond the fondest dreams of the course designer.

The matrix is also a valuable device for designing a PBL curriculum because it allows faculty members to translate what they have been teaching in their conventional curricula to PBL. They list all the important (not trivial) subject matter areas taught in each course down the left side. As patient problems are identified and added to the top of the matrix, the specific subject areas addressed are checked off. As the process continues, it is often seen that some content areas are not being addressed and particular effort will have to be taken to find a patient involving those areas. If a patient problem cannot be found, the relevance of that content area for medical student learning can be questioned.

This is a very logical way to choose problems for a PBL curriculum in medicine. For example, in a medical unit on cardiovascular and renal organ systems, the faculty determines the patient problems that will most likely be encountered by the students in their clinical courses, residencies, and in practice and includes these in the unit. This list of prevalent or common problems is augmented by cardiovascular or renal patient problems which, although not frequent, represent significant morbidity or mortality (and consequent financial burden to the health care system) if not recognized and properly managed. Then, whatever the students need to learn in the related basic sciences to evaluate, analyze, and manage these problems is the relevant content for self-directed study. An additional value to this curricular planning approach is that the curriculum is easily updated and kept relevant by adding new problems that surface in medicine. A similar strategy for developing a PBL curriculum could be applied in any technical or professional field.

Is Problem-Based Learning Worth the Trouble?

Interestingly, this question is usually raised by people who are asked to consider the possibility of a problem-based curriculum without having ever been involved in, or observing, problem-based learning. Once anyone is involved as a PBL tutor and has the opportunity of seeing what students can do when given the permission to think and learn on their own, he or she usually becomes a convert. Faculty members can see how students think, what they know, and how they are learning. This allows teachers to intervene early with students having trouble before it becomes a more difficult issue. Faculty members work with alert, motivated, turned-on minds in a collegial manner that has no equal. This is quite different from lecturing to a passive and often bored array of students whose understanding of the subject the teacher can only deduce indirectly from their answers to test questions.

The irony is that few formal assessment procedures can distinguish problem-based learning students from conventional curriculum students because such procedures are generally insensitive to the cognitive and behavioral differences that are observed in PBL. Yet faculty members who work with both conventional curriculum students and PBL students observe that there is a marked difference. There are two meta-evaluations that have pooled the results of many PBL evaluations performed over the last twenty years (Albanese and Mitchell, 1993; Vernon and Blake, 1993). These studies indicate that PBL has done no harm in terms of conventional tests of knowledge and that students may show better clinical problem-solving skills. They also show that students are stimulated and motivated by PBL as a method.

The proof is in the pudding. Teachers have to see problem-based learning in action, talk to students, and—most important—try it themselves. If they do this, concerns for evaluation diminish as they realize that PBL is a natural way for future doctors to learn.

Problem-Based Learning Outside the Medical Domain

Over the last two decades, PBL approaches and curricula have been developed in many other areas of education in professional schools (nursing, law, engineering), college-level courses, and kindergarten through 12th grade. Woods (1994) has developed PBL approaches in engineering at McMaster University for almost as many years as the medical school has existed. Stinson has developed an MBA program that is totally problem-based and introduced PBL into the final year of an undergraduate curriculum in business administration at Ohio University (Milter and Stinson, 1995). Gijselaers (1995) has developed a PBL curriculum in business at Maastricht. Boud and Felleti (1991) provide an excellent overview of the application of problem-based learning to many different disciplines.

More recently, Kelson and I have been working with high school teachers, initially in science, applying PBL to high school education. The Problem-Based Learning Institute, a cooperative venture between School District 186 in Springfield and Southern Illinois University School of Medicine, has developed problems and teacher-training programs in PBL for all the core disciplines in high school (Barrows and Kelson, 1993). The immediate interest in PBL shown by teachers after seeing it demonstrated, and the excitement shown by students and teachers who become involved, caused rapid dissemination. The method is perceived as the solution to many problems in education, such as the current tendency to produce students who cannot think or solve problems and who are bored with education.

As Internet list servers that support exchanges between those involved in problem-based learning reveal, there are many teachers using problem-based learning in many disciplines and professions and at many different educational levels around the world, and the numbers will grow as teachers see what PBL can accomplish.

References

Albanese, M. A., and Mitchell, S. "Problem-Based Learning: A Review of Literature on Its Outcomes and Implementation Issues." *Academic Medicine,* 1993, *68* (1), 52–81.

Barrows, H. S. "A Specific, Problem-Based, Self-Directed Learning Method Designed to Teach Medical Problem-Solving Skills, Self-Learning Skills and Enhance Knowledge Retention and Recall." In H. G. Schmidt and M. L. DeVolder (eds.), *Tutorials in Problem-Based Learning.* Assen/Maastricht, the Netherlands: Van Gorcum, 1984.

Barrows, H. S. "A Taxonomy of Problem-Based Learning Methods." *Medical Education,* 1986, *20,* 481–486.

Barrows, H. S. *Simulated (Standardized) Patients and Other Human Simulations.* Chapel Hill, N.C.: Health Sciences Consortium, 1987.

Barrows, H. S. *The Tutorial Process.* Springfield: Southern Illinois University School of Medicine, 1988.

Barrows, H. S. "Inquiry: The Pedagogical Importance of a Skill Central to Clinical Practice." *Medical Education,* 1990, *24,* 3–5.

Barrows, H. S. *Practice-Based Learning: Problem-Based Learning Applied to Medical Education.* Springfield: Southern Illinois University School of Medicine, 1994.

Barrows, H. S. "Problem-Based Learning and Problem Solving." *PROBE Newsletter of the Australian Problem-Based Learning Network,* 1996, *26,* 8–9.

Barrows, H. S., and Bennett, K. "The Diagnostic (Problem-Solving) Skill of the Neurologist." *Archives of Neurology,* 1972, *26,* 273–277.

Barrows, H. S., and Kelson, A. *Problem-Based Learning in Secondary Education and the Problem-Based Learning Institute* (Monograph). Springfield: Southern Illinois University School of Medicine, 1993.

Barrows, H. S., and Tamblyn, R. M. "The Portable Patient Problem Pack: A Problem-Based Learning Unit." *Journal of Medical Education,* 1977, *52* (12), 1002–1004.

Boud, D. J., and Felleti, G. (eds.). *The Challenge of Problem-Based Learning.* New York: St. Martin's Press, 1991.

Distlehorst, L. H., and Barrows, H. S. "A New Tool for Problem-Based Self-Directed Learning." *Journal of Medical Education,* 1982, *57* (6), 486–488.

Gijselaers, W. H. "Perspectives on Problem-Based Learning." In W. H. Gijselaers, D. T. Tempelaar, P. K. Keizer, J. M. Blommaert, E. M. Bernard, and H. Kasper (eds.), *Educational Innovation in Economics and Business Administration: The Case of Problem-Based Learning.* Norwell, Mass.: Kluwer, 1995.

Jones, J. W., Bieber, L. L., Echt, R., Scheifley, V., and Ways, P. O. "A Problem-Based Curriculum—Ten Years of Experience." In H. G. Schmidt and M. L. DeVolder (eds.), *Tutorials in Problem-Based Learning.* Assen/Maastricht, the Netherlands: Van Gorcum, 1984.

Levine, H. G., and Forman, P. B. "A Study of Retention of Knowledge of Neurosciences Information." *Journal of Medical Education,* 1973, *48* (9), 867–869.

Milter, R. G., and Stinson, J. E. "Educating Leaders for the New Competitive Environment." In W. H. Gijselaers, D. T. Tempelaar, P. K. Keizer, J. M. Blommaert, E. M. Bernard, and H. Kasper (eds.), *Educational Innovation in Economics and Business Administration: The Case of Problem-Based Learning.* Norwell, Mass.: Kluwer, 1995.

Muller, S. (Chair). "Physicians for the Twenty-First Century: Report of the Project Panel on the General Professional Education of the Physician and College Preparation for Medicine." *Journal of Medical Education,* 1984, *59* (11, Part 2).

Spaulding, W. B. "The Undergraduate Medical Curriculum (1969 Model): McMaster University." *Canadian Medical Association Journal,* 1969, *100,* 659–664.

Spaulding, W. B. "Revitalizing Medical Education." *McMaster Medical School in the Early Years, 1965–1974.* Philadelphia: Decker, 1991.

Vernon, D.T.A., and Blake, R. L. "Does Problem-Based Learning Work? A Meta-Analysis of Evaluative Research." *Academic Medicine,* 1993, *68* (7), 550–563.

Woods, D. R. *Problem-Based Learning: How to Gain the Most from PBL.* Waterdown: D. R. Woods, 1994. (Distributed by McMaster University Bookstore, Hamilton, Ontario, Canada.)

HOWARD S. BARROWS is professor and chair, department of medical education, Southern Illinois University School of Medicine, Springfield, Illinois.

*A framework for the analysis of problem-based learning methods
is presented, using concepts from cognitive psychology.*

Connecting Problem-Based Practices with Educational Theory

Wim H. Gijselaers

Problem-based learning (PBL) derives from the theory that learning is a process in which the learner actively constructs knowledge. Modern cognitive psychology suggests that learning results from a learner's actions and that instruction plays a role only to the extent that it enables and fosters constructive activities (Bereiter and Scardamalia, 1992). Transmission of subject-matter through direct instruction (lecturing, for example) is, from this perspective, only of limited use. If instruction is to play any role in the learning process, teachers should focus on helping students acquire self-directed learning skills.

Problem-based learning is regarded as an approach that meets this requirement (Schmidt, 1993). Problems serve as the stimulus for learning. Students encounter problem-solving situations in small groups that are guided by a tutor, whose role it is to facilitate the learning process by asking questions and monitoring the problem-solving process. This is quite different from most university teaching practices, which concentrate on the transmission of factual knowledge. PBL employs different instructional conditions to result in effective student learning (Norman and Schmidt, 1992). To create or improve PBL curricula, it is important to understand what kind of instructional conditions result in effective problem-based learning. This issue may be clarified by examining how the PBL method is grounded in current theories of learning and instruction and then by applying insights from these theories to refine the practice of problem-based learning.

The first section of this chapter describes certain fundamental principles of learning and instruction that are relevant to problem-based learning. The second section provides examples from the PBL process to illustrate how fundamental principles of cognition relate to instructional design in problem-

New Directions for Teaching and Learning, no. 68, Winter 1996 © Jossey-Bass Publishers

based learning. The final section looks at opportunities to improve the effects of problem-based learning on student learning.

Current Theories of Learning and Instruction

Findings from cognitive psychology provide a theoretical basis for improving instruction in general and problem-based learning in particular. A basic premise in cognitive psychology is that learning is a process of constructing new knowledge on the basis of current knowledge. According to Glaser (1991), it is generally assumed that learning is a constructive and not a receptive process, that cognitive processes called metacognition affect the use of knowledge, and that social and contextual factors influence learning.

Principle 1: Learning Is a Constructive and Not a Receptive Process. Until twenty or thirty years ago, education was dominated by the view that learning involves filling students' heads with information (Bruer, 1993). Human minds were regarded as empty buckets that could be filled through repetition and rehearsal. Accordingly, teaching led directly to students' storing knowledge in memory, like books are stored in libraries. Retrieving information depended on the quality of the call numbers used by students in classifying the information. However, modern cognitive psychology tells us that one of the most important features of memory is its associative structure (Bruer, 1993; Bruning, Schraw, and Ronning, 1995). Knowledge is structured in networks of related concepts, referred to as *semantic networks*. As learning occurs, new information is coupled to existing networks. Depending on how this is done by learners, new information may be effortlessly retrieved and used to solve problems, recognize situations, or recall factual knowledge.

Semantic networks are not only a way of storing information; they also influence how information is interpreted and recalled. For example, while reading a new text, certain passages will activate networks that contain existing knowledge needed to construct and retain the new text's meaning. If this does not occur, reading comprehension is inhibited. The following example illustrates this point. Read the passage once, then close the book, and write down as much as you can remember:

> The procedure is actually quite simple. First you arrange things into different groups. Of course, one pile may be sufficient depending on how much there is to do. If you have to go somewhere else, due to lack of facilities, that is the next step, otherwise you are pretty well set. It is important not to overdo things. That is, it is better to do a few things at once than too many [Bruer, 1993, p. 181; example adopted from Bransford and Johnson, 1972].

Bruer asserts that although the text in the example is quite simple, it is apt to be poorly understood. Most people read the passage slowly and focus for a long time on certain text parts. This process is generally regarded as seeking existing semantic networks that could interact with information in the text to construct meaning. If the title of this passage, "Washing Clothes," had been given first, the text would have been read rapidly and easily remembered. The title "Washing Clothes" activates existing knowledge related to information in the text. Consequently, in education, explicit attention should be paid to students' existing knowledge and the activation of this knowledge to provide a framework for learning. Activating existing knowledge to facilitate processing of new information is regarded as a basic requirement of learning.

Principle 2: Knowing About Knowing (or Metacognition) Affects Learning. A second important principle is that learning is quicker when students possess self-monitoring skills generally referred to as *metacognition* (Bruer, 1993). Metacognition is viewed as an essential element of skilled learning: goal-setting (What am I going to do?), strategy selection (How am I doing it?), and goal evaluation (Did it work?). Successful problem solving is not only dependent on the possession of an extensive body of knowledge, but also on the use of problem-solving methods to accomplish goals. According to Glaser (1991), several studies have shown that good students monitor their comprehension failures and successes while studying textbooks. Good students detect when they do—or do not—understand text and know when to use alternative strategies to understand learning materials. Typically, metacognitive skills include the ability to monitor one's own learning behavior, that is, being aware of how problems are analyzed and whether problem-solving results make sense. Studies of expert performance have shown that experts, in contrast with novices, constantly judge the difficulty of problems and assess their progress in resolving them (Glaser, 1991).

Some evidence exists that metacognition has to be developed in education, because monitoring of the learning process is usually late in developing (Bruning, Schraw, and Ronning, 1995). Fortunately many of these skills are teachable. Bruning, Schraw, and Ronning discuss several teaching strategies that can be used to teach metacognition: encourage students to engage in deep processing, focusing on understanding rather than surface memory; promote elaboration of new ideas; and help students become more metacognitively aware by demonstrating the kinds of questions they can ask themselves during problem-solving action.

Principle 3: Social and Contextual Factors Influence Learning. The third principle is about use of knowledge. Leading students to understand knowledge and to be able to use problem-solving processes are ambitious goals in higher education. Instruction typically begins by exposing students to disciplinary knowledge, and then assigning a series of end-of-chapter problems to promote the use of that knowledge.

Unfortunately, studies have shown that students experience serious difficulties in using scientific knowledge (Bruning, Schraw, and Ronning, 1995). Students also have erroneous beliefs about major principles in scientific disciplines. For example, studies have shown that traditional education does not facilitate an enhanced understanding of physics problems despite formally taught physics theories (for example, Clement, 1983). Similar results were found in economics education (Boshuizen, 1995). Indeed, research by Mandl, Gruber, and Renkl (1993) showed that psychology graduate students outperformed economics graduate students in a business simulation game. Graduate students in economics had the knowledge, but were unable to use it in a context that required fast and frequent decision making. On the other hand, psychology students had little knowledge of economics, but developed during the game a simple, partially incorrect, but effective decision-making model. Graduate students in economics used a complex model, but were unable to apply it during fast-paced problem-solving action. Mandl, Gruber, and Renkl (1993) found similar results with students in medicine. Medical students did not sufficiently relate signs and symptoms with the diagnoses formulated, ignored information that did not fit into their primary diagnosis, and were incapable of restructuring and synthesizing information presented in the case. According to Boshuizen (1995), numerous studies indicate that problems regarding the use of knowledge pervade higher education.

If our goal is to teach students to use their knowledge to solve real-world problems, then how should teaching occur? Mandl, Gruber, and Renkl (1993) propose a fourfold strategy to make university teaching more effective and resolve the problem of inert knowledge: instruction should be placed in the context of complex and meaningful problem-solving situations; instruction should focus on teaching metacognitive skills and when to use them; knowledge and skills should be taught from different perspectives and applied in many different situations; and instruction should take place in collaborative learning situations so as to confront students with beliefs held by other students. This strategy is based on two complementary models of contextualized learning: *cognitive apprenticeship* (Collins, Brown, and Newman, 1989) and *anchored instruction* (Bransford and others, 1990). Both models emphasize that teaching should take place in the context of real-world problems or professional practice (Williams, 1992). Cognitive apprenticeship emphasizes learning in the context in which students will perform when graduated. The major goal of apprentice learning is for students to see how experts use subject knowledge and metacognitive skills on a problem. Students need opportunities to see how experts analyze problems, to get feedback on their own actions, and to get suggestions during the process. In anchored instruction, students study concepts over an extended period of time in a variety of contexts. Through linking of content with context, knowledge becomes more accessible when confronting new problems (Schmidt, 1993).

Social factors also influence individual learning. Glaser (1991) argues that in small group work, the learner's exposure to alternative points of view is a real challenge to initial understanding. In small group work, students evoke their problem-solving methods and conceptual knowledge. They express their ideas and share responsibility in managing problem situations. Different views on a problem are observed, leading students to ask new questions. Bruning, Schraw, and Ronning (1995) argue that science instruction is more effective when the social nature of learning is recognized and used to help students acquire accurate scientific understanding.

Principles of Learning as Applied in Problem-Based Learning

Problem-based learning typically involves students working on problems in small groups of five to twelve with the assistance of a faculty tutor. Problems serve as the context for new learning. Their analysis and resolution result in the acquisition of knowledge and problem-solving skills. Problems are encountered before all relevant knowledge has been acquired and not only after reading texts or hearing lectures about the subject matter underlying a problem. This latter feature reflects one of the essential distinctions between problem-based learning and other problem-oriented methods (Albanese and Mitchell, 1993).

The problem-based tutor's function is to coach the group by providing support to make student interaction productive and to help students identify knowledge needed to resolve the problem. As a result of the problem-solving process, students generate questions (learning issues) about what kind of knowledge is required to explain the mechanisms underlying the causes of the problem. After leaving the meeting, students do research on the learning issues using a variety of resources. Significant time is available for independent study. The PBL process is completed when students report in the next meeting about what they have learned. The students' first goal is to relate newly acquired knowledge to the problem at hand. Their second focus is moving to a more general level of understanding, making transfer to new problems possible. After completing this problem-solving cycle, students will start to analyze a new problem, again following the analysis-research-report procedure.

Exhibit 2.1 contains an example of a first-year problem from the problem-based business program of the University of Limburg, Maastricht, the Netherlands. This problem is presented about three weeks after students have entered the business program. The problem is one in a series about how organizations should be structured and how they should formulate their organizational strategy given certain market demands.

Exhibit 2.1.   Example of a First-Year Problem

For more than fifty years, the Lee Company of Merriam, Kansas, did a good steady business. In the 1960s and 1970s, Lee Riders were riding high as jeans became fashionable among women as well as men. Lee couldn't make jeans fast enough. Recently, however, ten plants were closed down. Furthermore, Lee's international sales decreased despite enormous demand in foreign countries. Nowadays, Chief Executive Officer Fred Rowan is struggling to reorient Lee to suit the changes in the external environment. In order to make a sound reorientation, what is the first thing Fred should do?

Analysis of this problem takes place through several stages. The first step students take is to make sure everybody understands all the concepts and terms used in the problem. Students can raise questions about the concepts of organizational environment, dynamics of market behavior, and market share. Depending on their prior knowledge, students ask for more information about certain concepts in the Lee Company problem. This step serves an important purpose in the learning process. As discussed in the previous section, Principle 1 says that learning new information is based on existing knowledge. The first step of clarifying concepts elicits and activates existing knowledge. The primary analysis of the problem serves to activate prior knowledge, allowing students to couple new information to existing knowledge. Consequently, as the tutor listens, he or she gets information about students' existing knowledge and their naive beliefs about the mechanisms underlying the problem.

During the next step, students define and analyze the problem. For example, in discussing the problem, students may question why in a stage of growing market demand, Lee Company is not able to sell jeans. At this point, students are confronted with conflicting information: there is a substantial market demand; in the past, Lee was more or less surfing on market demands because production could not keep pace with demand; and now market demand is still growing, but Lee is unprofitable. This problem increases their interest in knowing more about organizational behavior and market analysis, because the information in the problem conflicts with their naive beliefs about market demand and opportunities to sell products, which say that if market demand is large, Lee Company should not have these problems.

At this stage, Principle 2 gains importance. A tutor who understands the role well will not tell students whether they are right or wrong in their thinking. The tutor resists giving the "right" solution. In the perspective of teaching metacognitive skills, a tutor asks questions that monitor the progress of problem-solving action (a process discussed in Chapter One). This models the kind of questions that students should be asking to identify the nature of the problem and the kind of knowledge required to understand it. These questions also lead students from the concrete problem and toward conceptual knowledge. Another important tutor role is to teach students how they can take on the role of expert. That is, the tutor asks students to reflect upon their own problem-solving behavior, and emphasizes that acquiring knowledge is a means, not an end. Knowledge is instrumental in the pursuit of competence in effectively managing problems.

As a result of discussing the problem, students study the relationships between the environment of an organization and organizational behavior. Possible learning issues are: How does the environment of organizations influence organizational behavior? What kind of organizational strategies are most effective given certain market features? How do you conduct a marketing opportunity analysis to determine how a company can be restructured in response to market demands?

The PBL process is completed when students report in a subsequent group session about what they have learned. At this stage, Principle 3 is important. Learning occurred because students were motivated by issues raised during the initial discussion of the problem. They wanted to understand the problem. When students report on what they have learned, the tutor provides feedback regarding whether the original learning issues have been resolved and whether students understand the issues behind the problem in sufficient depth. That is, ultimately teachers are not concerned with the problem encountered by Lee Jeans Company, but by the general issue of how market environments influence organizational behavior. Given that contextualization of knowledge is important to facilitate the use of knowledge, attention needs to be paid to both the particular case of Lee Jeans Company and to the general issue of market environment and organizational behavior. The particular case provides the context for learning new information and serves as a stepping-stone for students to acquire knowledge about the general problem domain. In this final stage of problem-based learning, the tutor may also demonstrate how conceptual knowledge about market environment and organizational behavior can be used to analyze the organizational behavior of other companies in different market environments. This enables students to observe how knowledge from one problem may be transferred to new problem situations.

Opportunities to Improve Problem-Based Learning

Insights from cognitive theories may help us manipulate the features of problem-based learning to improve learning. Williams (1992) points out that PBL is a relatively new and different form of education. Consequently, implementing problem-based learning is a difficult process. It is even more difficult to get the most out of its potential. Two essential features of problem-based learning seem to have a large impact on students' learning: the role of the tutor and the format of the problems (Albanese and Mitchell, 1993).

Role of the Tutor. As described in previous sections, a problem serves as the initiator of or stimulus for the learning process. Activation of prior knowledge through small group discussion is a key variable in this process. The tutor has to find a balance between allowing students to discuss issues and intervening to make sure that the critical learning issues are raised (Williams, 1992; Wilkerson, 1995). Our experience at the University of Limburg shows that this is very difficult for teachers. Without this balance, a tutor may be overly passive or may intervene in such a way as to stifle student discussion, for example giving minilectures, asking a constant stream of questions, giving answers, or providing literature references. Passive tutor behavior violates the first two learning principles that stress active construction of understanding and the importance of metacognitive skills. Rigid intervening behavior shifts the focus of the problem-based tutorial away from student-centered learning and toward teaching, ignoring the principle that learning is a constructive and not a receptive process. Recognizing that the tutor role is important, we need to include tutor development programs that stress how to realize active construction and metacognition.

Format of Problems. The second issue regards the format of problems. By this I do not mean the selection of problems, but the design of problems. Many different problem formats are in use in different programs. The design of effective problems is a painstaking process and few theory-based guidelines for problem construction are available in the literature (Schmidt, 1993; Gijselaers, 1995). This makes it difficult to develop principles for effective problem design. However, this issue may also be approached by asking the opposite question: what features of problem design may reduce the potential of problem-based learning? The following paragraphs contain some examples of ineffective problem design, based on experiences at the University of Limburg:

- *Ineffective problem descriptions include questions that are substituted for student-generated learning issue.* Students use these questions as benchmarks that should be reached after problem analysis. The process of problem-solving action turns into a process of backward reasoning because students know in advance what the outcomes should be.

- *The title of an ineffective problem is similar to titles of textbook chapters.* Teachers use titles to lead students and ensure that course objectives are covered. This situation may occur when teachers are afraid that students will not study what was initially intended, if left to themselves.

- *An ineffective problem does not result in motivation for self-study.* A problem may not contain a conflict in need of clarification or the problem may be too simple and can be completely resolved during the initial analytic process. This situation occurs when problems look like end-of-chapter exercises, or have only one acceptable solution and strategy for reaching it. Such problems are well-defined instead of ill-structured (Bruning, Schraw, and Ronning, 1995). The result may be that students restrict themselves to checking whether everyone got the same solution.

There is a growing awareness that problems are central to effective problem-based learning. At the University of Limburg, several studies have been conducted focusing on the link between problem design, students' initial problem analysis, and student learning. Dolmans (1994) demonstrated that students are quite capable of identifying those learning issues that faculty expect them to learn. However, she also found that students use other signals such as literature references, content in previous tests, and information from lectures in their decision-making about what to study and how to study. Dolmans (1994) recommends more research into how these factors interact with features of problems, which might add to our understanding of principles for effective problem design.

References

Albanese, M. A., and Mitchell, S. "Problem-Based Learning: A Review of Literature on Its Outcomes and Implementation Issues." *Academic Medicine,* 1993, *68* (1), 52–81.

Bereiter, C., and Scardamalia, M. "Cognition and Curriculum." In P. W. Jackson (ed.), *Handbook of Research on Curriculum*. Old Tappan, N.J.: Macmillan, 1992.

Boshuizen, H.A.P. "Teaching for Expertise." In W. H. Gijselaers, D. T. Tempelaar, P. K. Keizer, J. M. Blommaert, E. M. Bernard, and H. Kasper (eds.), *Educational Innovation in Economics and Business Administration: The Case of Problem-Based Learning*. Norwell, Mass.: Kluwer, 1995.

Bransford, J. D., and Johnson, M. K. "Contextual Prerequisites for Understanding: Some Investigations of Comprehension and Recall." *Journal of Verbal Learning and Verbal Behavior*, 1972, *11*, 717–726.

Bransford, J. D., Sherwood, R. D., Hasselbring, T. S., Kinzer, C. K., and Williams, S. M. "Anchored Instruction: Why We Need It and How Technology Can Help." In D. Nix and R. Spiro (eds.), *Cognition, Education, and Multimedia: Exploring Ideas in High Technology*. Hillsdale, N.J.: Erlbaum, 1990.

Bruer, J. T. *Schools for Thought: A Science of Learning in the Classroom*. Cambridge, Mass.: MIT Press, 1993.

Bruning, R. H., Schraw, G. J., and Ronning, R. R. *Cognitive Psychology and Instruction*. (2nd ed.) Englewood Cliffs, N.J.: Prentice Hall, 1995.

Clement, J. "A Conceptual Model Discussed by Galileo and Used Intuitively by Physics Students." In D. Gentner and A. L. Stevens (eds.), *Mental Models*. Hillsdale, N.J.: Erlbaum, 1983.

Collins, A., Brown, J. S., and Newman, S. "Cognitive Apprenticeship: Teaching the Crafts of Reading, Writing, and Mathematics." In L. B. Resnick (ed.), *Knowing, Learning, and Instruction: Essays in the Honor of Robert Glaser*. Hillsdale, N.J.: Erlbaum, 1989.

Dolmans, D. *How Students Learn in a Problem-Based Curriculum*. Maastricht, the Netherlands: Datawyse, Universitaire Pers, 1994.

Gijselaers, W. H. "Perspectives on Problem-Based Learning." In W. H. Gijselaers, D. T. Tempelaar, P. K. Keizer, J. M. Blommaert, E. M. Bernard, and H. Kasper (eds.), *Educational Innovation in Economics and Business Administration: The Case of Problem-Based Learning*. Norwell, Mass.: Kluwer, 1995.

Glaser, R. "The Maturing of the Relationship Between the Science of Learning and Cognition and Educational Practice." *Learning and Instruction*, 1991, *1*, 129–144.

Mandl, H. M., Gruber, H., and Renkl, A. "Das träge Wissen [Inert Knowledge]." *Psychologie Heute*, Sept. 1993, pp. 64–69.

Norman, G. R., and Schmidt, H. G. "The Psychological Basis of Problem-Based Learning: A Review of the Evidence." *Academic Medicine*, 1992, *67* (9), 557–565.

Schmidt, H. G. "Foundations of Problem-Based Learning: Some Explanatory Notes." *Medical Education*, 1993, *27*, 422–432.

Wilkerson, L. "Skills for the Problem-Based Tutor: Student and Faculty Perspectives." *Instructional Science*, 1995, *22*, 303–315.

Williams, S. M. "Putting Case-Based Instruction into Context: Examples from Legal and Medical Education." *Journal of the Learning Sciences*, 1992, *2* (4), 367–427.

WIM H. GIJSELAERS is associate professor in the department of educational development and educational research at the University of Limburg, Maastricht, the Netherlands.

*Group size, teacher skills, problem types, and student behaviors are
central concerns to PBL planners and teachers. In implementing
problem-based curricula, decisions about each of these dimensions
have implications for the others.*

Tutors and Small Groups in Problem-Based Learning: Lessons from the Literature

LuAnn Wilkerson

Picture this scenario: The session began with a question from the faculty tutor about issues encountered in their self-study since beginning the problem in tutorial on Friday. In response, Bill asked about the action of catecholamines. This led into a discussion of high versus low output cardiac failure in this patient and the relationship to her possible thyroid disease. After an obvious pause in the flow of the discussion, the tutor asked Cal if he would explain his earlier suggestion that this patient's cardiac problems might be best explained by a diagnosis of hyperthyroidism. Most of the remainder of the session consisted of a discussion among five of the six students present of thyroxin, thyroglobulin binding protein, and mechanisms of various treatments, particularly as complicated by cardiac disease. Three of the students offered elaborate explanations and the faculty tutor participated frequently by asking questions to follow up on these explanations or by adding brief comments from his clinical experience and recent reading. Donna suggested that they needed to learn more about adrenal function in thyroid disease.

What is going on in this problem-based tutorial? From the experience of group facilitators in PBL, we know that students do most of the talking and tutors do a lot of listening. What is the nature of that talk? How does the content and format of the problem contribute to the nature of the talk and the interaction? Is tutorial leadership or group interaction related to student learning? Studies of problem-based learning (PBL) in the health professions provide some insight into each of these questions. In this article, I will present a model for analyzing features of educational groups, use this model to review a few key studies of PBL groups and tutors that I have found most helpful in my role as a curriculum planner and faculty developer, and identify issues for discussion and study.

A Model of Small Group Interaction in Educational Settings

Of particular interest to the topic of tutors and small groups is research by Hertz-Lazarowitz on schoolwide transitions from traditionally structured to cooperatively structured learning. She and her colleagues (Hertz-Lazarowitz and Miller, 1992) bring together research from education, developmental psychology, and social psychology to illuminate the dynamic processes fundamental to group interaction and its outcomes. Based on ten years of research in education at both the University of Southern California and the University of Haifa in Israel and her work in introducing schools at all levels to cooperative learning structures, she has developed a model for analyzing the multiple dimensions of classroom groups and the interrelationships between classroom patterns and the social and academic behaviors of learners. Figure 3.1 presents her six-dimensional model of classroom interaction, which combines four process variables—organizational structure, learning task, teacher's instructional behavior, and teacher's communicative behavior—with two outcome variables, student's academic behavior and student's social behavior.

Hertz-Lazarowitz has labeled the model *mirrors of the classroom* because "the dimensions that characterize the classroom setting are interrelated; structures and activities in one dimension are reflected in each dimension." (p. 73). The mirrors model has served as the theoretical framework for her research on interactive classrooms from elementary to adult education. To date, the little research that has been done on the interactions of tutors and students in problem-based classrooms has been done in medical education at a few institutions and generally without the cohesiveness of a guiding theory.

Classroom Organizational Structure

Every group has some type of organizational structure. In problem-based learning, group size and configuration differ from school to school. What is the best size for PBL groups? Group size usually comes down to who is available to serve as tutors, how many students there are, and how many tutors can be recruited and how many rooms located. Most PBL programs prefer groups of eight or less. Hare (1962) reviews the results of numerous studies on the relationship of group size to a range of outcome variables. He concludes that five members is the most productive size for a small discussion group. Participants have reported less satisfaction with smaller groups in which each member may have to take a prominent role or larger groups in which there is limited opportunity to speak.

These general findings from the communication literature are borne out

Figure 3.1. Six Mirrors of the Classroom

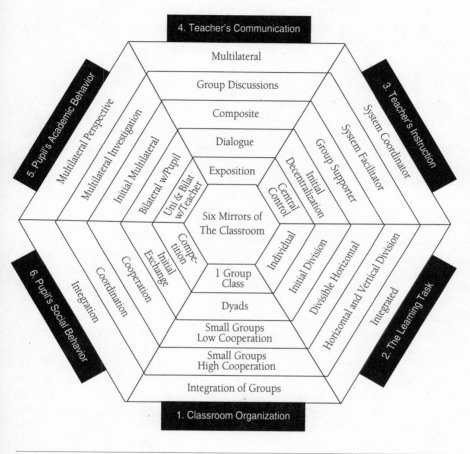

Source: Hertz-Lazarowitz and Miller, 1992, p. 74. Copyright © 1992 by Cambridge University Press. Reprinted with the permission of Cambridge University Press.

in a recent qualitative study by Burns and Keller (1995), in which thirteen first-year medical students were interviewed and observed during a Gross Anatomy PBL course. A portion of time was spent in one large group with a faculty tutor and a portion in two small groups with the tutor moving between the two groups. Students reported that the smaller group allowed more opportunity for participation and therefore required more preparation. They found student-to-student discussion was essential as they depended on one another for clarification and elaboration more than in the larger group, in which one or two students competed for the attention of the tutor. Finally, the students felt the discussion was more focused in the smaller group with more time to go into depth on a topic and to consider the most interesting aspects of a problem.

Another structural issue concerns group composition. Do tutorial groups need a faculty tutor every time? De Grave, De Volder, Gijselaers, and Damoi-seaux (1990) compared test scores with students' ratings of group functioning and tutor behaviors in PBL groups with student versus staff tutors. There was no difference in achievement between conditions. Students rated the tutorials as equally productive and participation as equivalent, although their ratings indicated that peer and faculty tutors used different behaviors in tutorial. Faculty tutors behaved more like experts while student tutors behaved more like colleagues. Our experience with first- and second-year medical students at the University of California, Los Angeles, suggests that groups can meet on their own without a faculty member present when beginning a new problem and still arrive at the majority of the learning objectives identified as important (Duek, Wilkerson, and Adinolfi, 1996).

The Learning Task

The problem serves as the initial stimulus and framework for learning in PBL. Problems can range from a single phenomenon in need of an explanation to a complex simulation that unfolds in response to students' questions, usually posed to a computer, the faculty tutor, or (in medicine) a patient, either real or simulated. When is a more focused, structured problem useful and when is a more complex, ill-structured problem useful? What is the relationship between the structure of a problem and students' academic behaviors or tutors' instructional behaviors?

In a review of research on the conditions for productive small group learning, Cohen (1994) concluded "that the relationship of the total amount of interaction within a group to achievement differs according to the nature of the task" (Cohen, 1994, p. 3). The use of tasks with clear procedures and right answers was associated with limited exchange of information among students, the generation of simple explanations, and routine learning. More ill-structured, complex tasks provoked extended elaboration among group members and were associated with conceptual learning.

Two studies in medical education have demonstrated a relationship between the degree of structure in the curriculum, tutors' content expertise, and levels of student achievement. Schmidt (1994) found that tutor expertise was unrelated to achievement in those health science courses at the University of Limburg rated by students as well-structured or for which their prior knowledge was high. In a study of the discussion of a single case in an otherwise traditional medical microbiology course, Davis and others (1994) from the University of Michigan School of Medicine found that when the case material was focused and the intended learning objectives were clearly communicated to the tutors, the tutor's expertise was unrelated to students' scores on a relevant multiple choice test. However, tutors with extensive expertise in the subject of the case engaged in more teacher-directive behaviors while their students exhibited fewer initiation behaviors than in tutorials led by more generalist faculty. As Hertz-Lazarowitz suggests (1992), classroom dimensions are a reflection of one another.

To what extent do different groups working on the same problem learn the same things? How much overlap exists between the learning issues identified by students and those intended by the faculty in its design of a problem? Dolmans, Gijselaers, Schmidt, and Van der Meer (1993) studied the amount of overlap in a second-year medical school course at the University of Limburg. Each tutorial group identified 85 percent of the fifty-one faculty objectives for the twelve problems in the course. Looking at each problem, there was immense variability in overlap, ranging from 28 percent to 100 percent. The problem with 100 percent was brief and contained few objectives, that is, it was well-structured.

Teacher Instructional Behavior

What instructional skills are needed by PBL tutors? In my own study of the ratings of first-year medical students at Harvard Medical School (Wilkerson, 1995), students were asked to describe the ways in which tutors were most helpful in promoting learning. Those tutors receiving the highest overall ratings were most often described as engaging in the following behaviors. Quotes taken from students' written comments illustrate each of these behaviors.

- *Balancing student-direction with assistance.* "He let the students in the tutorial have free rein to guide the course of study, but always held us accountable to a critical thought process." "His intervention/contributions specifically serve to focus and summarize and enhance, and not to exert control."
- *Contributing knowledge and experience.* "The importance of basic science to clinical medicine was emphasized repeatedly, which was an encouragement for me to study the stuff." "Bringing in extra readings, adding information from his own research and clinical experience, obviously working hard at keeping up with what's going on in our course."
- *Creating a pleasant learning environment.* "Responded to very diverse points of view, styles, and scientific preparation equally enthusiastically. No one felt left out." "Lowering tensions in a fairly hostile group such that by the end of the block, the group interacted exquisitely."
- *Stimulating critical evaluation of ideas.* "Gets us to think, reason, and question everything we see, hear about, or read in books." "Often forced us to look, from a different perspective, at issues we thought we had figured out so that we could discover how much more complex things are than we sometimes think."

Using end-of-course questionnaires completed by students in 524 different tutorial groups, Schmidt and Moust (1995) found support for a complex model of tutor, group, and study-time interactions. They introduce two new concepts helpful in understanding the role of the tutor. The first, *social congruence,* is a measure of the tutor's liking for and interest in the students. The second, *cognitive congruence,* describes the ability of the tutor to "express oneself in the language of the students, using the concepts they use and explaining things in ways easily grasped by students" (p. 709). The resulting model suggests three interrelated qualities in an effective tutor: an attitude of caring for and interest in the students, a knowledge base relevant to the learning objectives of the course, and the ability to translate this knowledge into terms readily accessible by students. These three characteristics exert a direct and indirect influence on tutorial group functioning and hence on intrinsic interest in the subject matter and time spent in self-study, and thus on achievement on examinations.

The Hertz-Lazarowitz model suggests that tutors' instructional behaviors need to be studied in the context of the content to be learned and other classroom dimensions, a point raised in a provocative paper by Gijselaers (1994) showing that the same tutor exhibits different behaviors when tutoring in different courses.

Teacher Communicative Behavior

In a survey of 822 experienced PBL tutors from twenty-two North American medical schools (Vernon, 1995), faculty tutors indicated that the best aspects of PBL were tutor-student relationships, student motivation, group atmosphere, and student-directed learning. What tutor behaviors encourage this type of learning environment? Some faculty members believe that remaining silent is the essential communication behavior. To explore this perception, my colleagues and I (Wilkerson, Hafler, and Liu, 1991) used qualitative research methods to study the patterns of interaction among the four PBL tutors and twenty-four medical students in a second-year pathophysiology course. Two distinct patterns of interaction emerged. *Student-directed discussion* was characterized by students' selection of the topics for discussion, tutors' contributions that built on students' previous comments, tutors' questions that served to guide group process and probe thinking, long runs of student-to-student discussion, and frequent periods of silence. In contrast, *tutor-directed discussion* involved the tutor suggesting topics and arguing or interrupting when students suggested topics. Tutors' comments in the latter model were slightly more frequent, with more teacher-student-teacher interactions. These tutors used questions to raise new topics or request specific information. In the interviews, both groups of tutors explained these behaviors through reference to their own beliefs about group discussion and student expectations. There was no difference in the amount of tutor talk between the student-directed and tutor-directed groups.

Davis and his colleagues (1992, 1994) used Flanders Interaction Analysis to determine the percent of time spent by tutors and students in ten behaviors. In their initial study, they found no difference in tutor and student behaviors under conditions of expertise and nonexpertise. In the replication study, with a more focused case and supportive tutor materials, the expert tutors increased their directed behaviors while student initiation behaviors decreased, creating a significant difference between expert and nonexpert groups.

We need more studies of groups at work using both quantitative and qualitative methodologies. Our understanding of teachers' communication and instructional behaviors could be enhanced by focusing future research on multiple dimensions of the mirrors model.

Student Academic Behavior

Academic skills are one of the outcomes that we are seeking to influence in PBL. These skills include behaviors engaged in by students during tutorial interactions and periods of self-directed study. Studies in PBL have included such academic outcomes as time spent in self-study, use of library resources, progress tests, course examinations, types of explanations given in tutorial, and aspects of scientific reasoning demonstrated in discussion.

What resources do PBL students use? In a cross-institutional survey of second-year medical students from four medical schools, Rankin (1992) found that PBL students were more likely to use journals and computerized bibliographic searches than were traditional students, who relied more often on faculty members. The PBL students predicted that on-line searching would be their most useful resource once they were in practice; traditional students thought colleagues would be their primary source of information.

In a comparative study of the continuing education practices of medical graduates of a PBL and a traditional medical school in Canada, Shin, Haynes, and Johnston (1993) found that in keeping up with the latest recommendations for hypertension, PBL graduates were significantly more likely to know current treatment recommendations and were better able to distinguish successful approaches to enhancing compliance than traditional graduates.

What academic behaviors in tutorial are related to performance on examinations? I have been particularly interested in the types of explanations that students give to one another after periods of self-study. Research by Chi (1989) and Webb (1992) on the role of elaboration in learning suggest that the giving of elaborated explanations to oneself during self-study or during small group discussions is a powerful predictor of subsequent achievement. What types of explanations do students give in PBL? What is the effect of different types of tasks on the type and amount of elaboration given? What tutor communication and instructional behaviors are associated with the students' giving of elaborations? At UCLA, we are studying the types of explanations given by the same students in a PBL course with a basic science focus and one with a social medicine focus.

Dolmans (1994) explored the relationship between students' self-generated learning issues, overlap with the faculty's objectives, and reported study time. Students in a second-year medical course were asked to assess their mastery of each major topic in the course and to indicate how much time they had spent studying each topic. Time and mastery correlations for the twelve problems in the course ranged from .46 to .89, with a mean correlation of .69. "What students plan to do, as expressed in the list of learning issues produced after problem discussion, is essentially unrelated to what they actually do" (p. 262). In a cross-sectional survey of 407 medical students in years one to four at the University of Limburg, Dolmans and Schmidt (1994) found that first-year students were more influenced by the content to be tested, the lectures, and the reference literature citations than more advanced students. Discussion in the tutorial group remained a constant stimulus to self-study across the years and emerged as the most important stimulus by year three.

Student Social Behaviors

Social skills are an important component in small group discussion as students engage in the exchange of ideas, the construction of meaning, and the interplay of personalities. Interaction requires skills in listening, soliciting opinions, encouraging explicitness, highlighting differences of opinion, synthesizing viewpoints, and cooperating in the execution of a task. Hertz-Lazarowitz (1992) has studied two types of cooperation—low and high. Both occur in PBL. In low cooperation, each student researches his or her own learning issue, then comes to the return tutorial to present the results to the group. A round of minilectures ensues. In high cooperation, students engage in discussion, clarification, and feedback as they bring their individual work back to the group. Carr (described in Koschmann and others, 1995) examined the quality and quantity of verbal discourse in two PBL medical schools. She found that the types and amounts of participation were similar in both schools. She also found that the student seated directly across from the tutor spoke the most frequently and for the longest period of time, a finding that agrees with other group process research. The most frequently exhibited cognitive behavior by students was exposition, which occupied 49 percent of the tutorial.

Using the mirrors model, we might next wonder how students' verbal interactions are related to other dimensions. Davis and his colleagues (1994) have provided a brief glimpse into the relationship between the tutors' content expertise, the tutors' communicative behaviors, and student discourse. Silver and Wilkerson (1991) compared the verbal interactions among students and between the students and the tutor in discussions of topics in which the tutor was a self-identified expert and those in which he or she was not. In addition to these, there are many more questions in search of a study.

In her review of the conditions for productive small groups, Cohen (1994) concludes that complex, verbalized thinking and social skills will not be displayed automatically by students who are part of cooperative learning groups. Without explicit training in discourse and social skills, small groups appear to operate at the most concrete level. If this same phenomenon holds with students in higher education, we need to teach students the social behaviors associated with productive group discussions.

Summary

The mirrors model provides a framework for the development and evaluation of PBL activities in courses across the higher education spectrum, although much of the research to date has occurred in medical and other health science schools. The model is helpful in organizing the disparate research and evaluation agenda of the members of the PBL community into a coherent body of work on tutors and small groups. It also serves as a reminder that decisions about group size, learning tasks, and tutor behaviors need to be examined in the context of other classroom dimensions and environmental features outside of the classroom. The context serves as a guide for designing orientation and development programs for students and faculty. If we consider the various levels of structure and activity that Hertz-Lazarowitz includes in each dimension, the model is useful in judging the degree to which a new PBL curriculum has moved away from traditional instruction. The model is a constant reminder that when changing one dimension of a course or even a single tutorial, we need to be watching for the reflections of that change in the multiple dimensions inherent in the situation. I am hoping to be less surprised and more observant as a result.

References

Burns, D., and Keller, J. L. "An Effective Solution for the Increasing Mismatch Between Faculty Resources and the Optimal Size of PBL Groups." Poster presented at the Research in Medical Education annual meeting, Washington, D.C., Nov. 1995.

Chi, M.T.H., Bassok, M., Lewis, M. W., Reimann, P., and Glaser, R. "Self-Explanations: How Students Study and Use Examples in Learning to Solve Problems." *Cognitive Science,* 1989, *13,* 145–182.

Cohen, E. G. "Restructuring the Classroom: Conditions for Productive Small Groups." *Review of Educational Research,* 1994, *64* (1), 1–35.

Davis, W. K., Nairn, R., Paine, M. E., Anderson, R. M., and Oh, M. S. "Effects of Expert and Non-Expert Facilitators on the Small-Group Process and on Student Performance." *Academic Medicine,* 1992, *67,* 470–474.

Davis, W. K., Nairn, R., Paine, M. E., Anderson, R. M., and Oh, M. S. "Influence of a Highly Focused Case on the Effect of Small-Group Facilitators' Content Expertise on Students' Learning and Satisfaction." *Academic Medicine,* 1994, *69* (8), 663–669.

De Grave, W. S., De Volder, M. L., Gijselaers, W. H., and Damoiseaux, V. "Peer Teaching and Problem-Based Learning: Tutor Characteristics, Tutor Functioning, Group Functioning, and Student Achievement." In Z. M. Nooman, H. G. Schmidt, and E. S. Ezzat (eds.), *Innovation in Medical Education: An Evaluation of Its Present Status.* New York: Springer, 1990.

Dolmans, D.H.J.M., Gijselaers, W. H., Schmidt, H. G., and Van der Meer, S. B. "Problem Effectiveness in a Course Using Problem-Based Learning." *Academic Medicine,* 1993, *68* (3), 207–213.

Dolmans, D.H.J.M., and Schmidt, H. G. "What Drives the Student in Problem-Based Learning?" *Medical Education,* 1994, *28* (5), 372–380.

Dolmans, D.H.J.M., Schmidt, H. G., and Gijselaers, W. H. "The Relationship Between Student-Generated Learning Issues and Self-Study in Problem-Based Learning." *Instructional Science,* 1994, *22* (4), 251–267.

Duek, J. E., Wilkerson, L., and Adinolfi, T. "Learning Issues Identified by Students in Tutor-less Problem-Based Tutorials." *Advances in Health Sciences Education,* 1996, *1* (1), 29–40.

Gijselaers, W. H. "Analysis of Tutor Behavior at Different Time Points and Within Different Departments." Paper presented at the American Educational Research Association annual meeting, New Orleans, Apr. 1994.

Hare, A. P. *Handbook of Small Group Research.* New York: Free Press, 1962.

Hertz-Lazarowitz, R. "Understanding Interactive Behaviors: Looking at Six Mirrors of the Classroom." In R. Hertz-Lazarowitz and N. Miller (eds.), *Interaction in Cooperative Groups: The Theoretical Anatomy of Group Learning.* New York: Cambridge University Press, 1992.

Hertz-Lazarowitz, R., and Miller, N. (eds.). *Interaction in Cooperative Groups: The Theoretical Anatomy of Group Learning.* New York: Cambridge University Press, 1992.

Koschmann, T., Carr, L. L., Conlee, M., Kalishman, S., and Wilkerson, L. "Looking and Listening: Understanding Small Group Process in a Problem-Based Learning Meeting." Symposium presented at the American Educational Research Association annual meeting, San Francisco, Apr. 1995.

Rankin, J. A. "Problem-Based Medical Education: Effect on Library Use." *Bulletin of the Medical Library Association,* 1992, *80* (1), 36–43.

Schmidt, H. G. "Resolving Inconsistencies in Tutor Expertise Research: Does Lack of Structure Cause Students to Seek Tutor Guidance?" *Academic Medicine,* 1994, *69* (8), 656–662.

Schmidt, H. G., and Moust, J.H.C. "What Makes a Tutor Effective? A Structural-Equation Modeling Approach to Learning in Problem-Based Curricula." *Academic Medicine,* 1995, *7* (8), 708–714.

Shin, J. H., Haynes, R. B., and Johnston, M. E. "Effect of Problem-Based, Self-Directed Undergraduate Education on Life-Long Learning." *Canadian Medical Association Journal,* 1993, *148* (6), 969–976.

Silver, M., and Wilkerson, L. "Effects of Tutors with Subject Expertise on the Problem-Based Tutorial Process." *Academic Medicine,* 1991, *66* (5), 298–300.

Vernon, D.T.A. "Attitudes and Opinions of Faculty Tutors About Problem-Based Learning." *Academic Medicine,* 1995, *70* (3), 216–223.

Webb, N. "Testing a Theoretical Model of Student Interaction and Learning in Small Groups." In R. Hertz-Lazarowitz and N. Miller (eds.), *Interaction in Cooperative Groups: The Theoretical Anatomy of Group Learning.* New York: Cambridge University Press, 1992.

Wilkerson, L. "Identification of Skills for the Problem-Based Tutor: Student and Faculty Perspectives." *Instructional Science,* 1995, *23* (4), 303–315.

Wilkerson, L., Hafler, J. P., and Liu, P. "A Case Study of Student-Directed Discussion in Four Problem-Based Groups." *Academic Medicine,* 1991, *66* (9 Supplement), S79–S81.

LUANN WILKERSON is associate dean for medical education and director of the Center of Educational Development and Research at the University of California, Los Angeles, School of Medicine.

Drawing on eleven years' experience with a problem-based learning MBA program, we have found that the way in which the PBL process is used, faculty capabilities, and student transition are critical implementation issues.

Problem-Based Learning in Business Education: Curriculum Design and Implementation Issues

John E. Stinson, Richard G. Milter

This chapter is based on our experience implementing problem-based learning in the Ohio University Masters in Business Administration (MBA) program. We have moved from a traditional course-based, discipline-divided MBA to a completely problem-based program during the last eleven years. We started without a road map and made many mistakes along the way. But we also gained some insights that may be of use to others attempting to implement problem-based learning. It is in this spirit that we share our story.

Defining the Goals of the Ohio University MBA

The Ohio University MBA presently is an intense thirteen-month learning experience, starting in August of year one and concluding in September of year two. There are also part-time programs housed at our regional campuses. These distance learning programs are lockstep cohort programs requiring approximately two and a half years to complete.

All programs use a problem-based learning format with a theoretical base in cognitive constructivism, a format that places the learner in exactly the type of projects and work situations that he or she will face as a leader of the information age organizations of the twenty-first century. Students learn basic business concepts, but in the context of use, maximizing their ability to both recall and apply those concepts as they move back into the work world. Students develop the skills (communication, collaboration, teamwork) and the personal characteristics (initiative, creativity, personal responsibility) that are becoming

NEW DIRECTIONS FOR TEACHING AND LEARNING, no. 68, Winter 1996 © Jossey-Bass Publishers

necessary for success. Students develop a high level of comfort with information technology as they regularly access information through the resources of the Internet, collaborate electronically over time and space, and develop and make professional-level, computer-driven presentations.

The program centers around eight major projects. The projects tend to be large macro problems that address business holistically. There are, within any project, multiple smaller problems that students must address to manage the total learning problem. Students construct their knowledge of business practices by working their way through the problems. Student learning is aided by the ability to access appropriate content on a just-in-time basis. Students learn content at a time when it will be most useful to them in their management of the learning problems. While some of the problems are designed to challenge individuals separately, most of them are designed to be approached by collaborative learning groups.

The problem-based learning process employed is a derivative of Reiterative Problem-Based Learning, which was developed by Barrows (1985) and follows closely the concepts of cognitive constructivism (Savery and Duffy, 1994) and cognitive apprenticeship (Brown, Collins, and Duguid, 1989). For a more complete description of our use of the action learning process, see Stinson (1990) and Milter and Stinson (1995).

Developing the Curriculum

Our first movement into a more integrated curriculum using PBL was prompted by criticism of graduate business education. In the early eighties, business schools were chastised by the popular press for being too theoretical and out of touch with business realities, for producing narrow-minded technicians without interpersonal and communication skills, and for concentrating on esoteric research unrelated to the business world.

While some of the reports were sensationalized and demonstrated a lack of understanding of both business schools and the business world, there was merit to the concerns expressed. Many business schools, including ours, heard from members of their executive advisory boards that graduates were not well prepared for the business world. Board members noted that graduates did not have a realistic understanding of the business world; they criticized graduates for ineffective communication skills; they noted the lack of leadership skills; and they commented on the need to train new graduates, teaching them concepts they supposedly learned in school. Similar concerns were expressed in the Business–Higher Education Forum in its May 1985 report to President Reagan, *America's Business Schools: Priorities for Change.*

In response to those concerns, we performed a complete redesign of our curriculum. The redesign process was conducted by an interdisciplinary team who formed the central delivery team for the program. On this team were faculty from each major discipline in the College.

The process began by attempting to establish desired student outcomes. To approach that issue, we asked ourselves, "What is it that we want our students to know, and know how to do, as they leave our program?" We attempted to answer the question from three different perspectives:

• Each discipline-based participant was asked to draw upon his or her technical expertise and propose what were the minimum acceptable conceptual knowledge and skills that all MBA graduates (not discipline majors) should have from their area. Each participant then had to defend the resulting list to the other faculty representing other disciplines.

• Businesspeople who might be expected to hire graduates of MBA programs were polled. They were asked what they expected incoming recent graduates to know and to know how to do.

• A futures analysis was performed. Given that our job is to prepare people to assume leadership roles in business in the future, we wanted to make certain that we were helping students develop the types of knowledge and skills that provide a base for long-term, as well as short-term, success.

We employed this process during our last major redesign in 1992 and have performed the same analysis in abbreviated form each year since. We reinvent the program each year; it is never conducted exactly the same way twice. Using this process, we have developed a dozen desired student outcomes. Under each of these outcomes, called *meta-outcomes,* we have developed a more specific set of learning outcomes (approximately 150) that drive the structure of the program.

The meta-outcomes are much broader than those traditionally identified for MBA programs. In addition to knowledge and the ability to apply the knowledge, they incorporate a number of skills and personal characteristics. Because of the breadth and the interrelatedness of those outcomes, we concluded some time ago that a typical discipline-based and course-structured curriculum would not produce the desired outcomes.

Further, as constructivist research shows (Duffy and Jonassen, 1991), positivist pedagogues encourage the development of personal characteristics counter to those we needed to develop. For example, in the more positivist-based pedagogy, students are encouraged to be passive. Our outcomes, on the other hand, call for them to become active initiators. Traditionally, the faculty has taken responsibility for providing clarity to students. Our outcomes call for students to clarify their own roles in ambiguous situations. Thus we concluded that a pedagogy based on a constructivist philosophy of learning, problem-based learning, was more appropriate given our desired learning outcomes.

We have now had over a decade of experience implementing problem-based learning. While some may still have concerns about the effectiveness of the process, we do not. Rather, our concerns center on the implementation of problem-based learning. Inappropriately used, problem-based learning will not lead to the potential robust learning. It is our experience that the critical implementation issues, those that may actually limit learning, include incomplete or inappropriate use of the process, faculty capabilities and attitudes, and issues of student transition.

Designing Problems and Extracting Learning

The design and implementation of appropriate problems is central to effective problem-based learning. Although problem-situations may be somewhat similar to traditional cases in business, they emphasize both the acquisition of information and the structuring of the situation to permit analysis. In the traditional case format, each of these activities is carried out by the case writer and affords no opportunity for student learning of valuable skills.

We agree with Schank and Cleary (1995) that, too frequently, inadequate attention is given to the design of problems. In our experience, there has been a tendency by less experienced faculty members to select a problem because it is convenient or interesting. The tendency is to then fudge the development of learning outcomes to fit the selected problem. This, of course, is inappropriate. Effective problem design begins with a set of clearly identified learning outcomes. It is the learning outcomes that should drive problem design, and not the other way around.

What are good problems? In their description of goal-based scenarios, Schank and Cleary (1995) note that problems should be both authentic and engaging. Barrows (1985) proposes that problems should be ill-structured. Consistent with these guidelines and drawing upon the constructivist philosophy, we have developed a number of principles that guide our development of problems and projects. These principles follow.

Learning Outcomes Should be Holistic, Not Divided by Narrow Disciplinary Boundaries. Focusing on content only within narrow disciplinary boundaries limits potential learning. Further, disciplinary boundaries are largely a construct of academic convenience. In practice, there is no such thing as a "marketing problem." Any action taken in the marketing area of the firm impinges on the operational area and the financial area. As firms today are learning the importance of becoming more boundaryless and organizing around processes designed to serve customers, learning outcomes need to become more boundaryless as well.

Problems Should Mirror Professional Practice. This meets the criterion of authenticity. Problems should be similar in nature to the problems we find in professional practice or at least call forth the same types of skills and activities. Thus, content will be learned in the context of practice so that, when needed for practice, the content can be more readily recalled and used. More and more over time, as the student confronts and manages authentic situations, the process of learning and doing becomes intertwined and indivisible. The learner manager develops the ability and accepts the responsibility for managing his or her own learning. The manager in practice approaches each situation as a learning experience and has the ability to reflect upon experience and extract knowledge that will lead to continual growth in capability. The learner manager will evolve into the learning manager.

Problems Should be Ill-Structured. In practice, managers are seldom confronted with neat, well-structured problems. Rather, they most frequently face what Ackoff (1979) has characterized as "managerial messes." Students need to develop the ability to confront ambiguous, ill-defined situations and make sense of them. They need to be able to recall concepts and techniques and apply them in this sense-making process. Further, they need to engage in and develop an effective inquiry process. There is no textbook or written case study for this process.

Once again, this is authentic. The information needed to analyze a situation is not prepackaged, preanalyzed, and provided for the manager. There is no "Harvard Business School Case Study" of the day. Managers must be able to determine what information is needed and to obtain and interpret the information. By repeatedly confronting and managing ill-structured problems, students develop the ability to ask the right questions and to determine what information is needed to frame the situation. Further, they learn where and how to obtain the needed information. They develop the truly requisite business research skills.

Problems Should be Contemporary. While authenticity is emphasized in all these principles, engagement is implied. In our experience, authentic problems are engaging. Students see such problems as real and find them stimulating to attack. But these stimulating real problems should also be contemporary. Students are not engaged by a challenge to determine what a company should have done ten years ago. This is a typical problem of Harvard-type cases. Students do not accept the authenticity of a case set several years in the past and thus are not engaged. An additional problem with an historic case is a search for the right answer. This gives students an impression that complex business problems are simply puzzles requiring selection of the correct responses.

Learning from the Problems

While design of problems is critical, effective implementation is also essential. In particular, students must learn from their experience and be able to generalize from the specific situation to more robust knowledge and understanding.

Albanese and Mitchell (1993) note that graduates of problem-based medical programs sometimes report a lack of confidence that they have learned as much content as have those who went through a traditional program. They further note research that sought to measure extent of content learning. They conclude that research suggests somewhat less knowledge among problem-based learning graduates. Note, however, that this conclusion reflects a measurement bias. It is based on measurement of learning via standardized objective tests. Measures more directly related to professional activity, that is, data from evaluations of clinical performance were discounted—because "clinical evaluation represents a complex mix of personal and secondary observation of residents" (p. 77). This bias causes us to question the validity of the conclusion. Rather than suggesting a weakness in the concept of problem-based learning as was implied, these reviews may suggest a weakness in the implementation of the learning process.

In our early use of problem-based learning, we experienced similar concerns. Students would learn, but would exit the program not fully comprehending how much they had learned. Further, they could not effectively access their learning in nonassociated recall and thus could not demonstrate the extent of their learning on traditional tests.

A review of our use of problem-based learning revealed that we were not effectively helping students to make their learning explicit. We were assuming that the students would, as a natural part of the learning process, reflect on their experience and extract abstract knowledge. At most, we would conduct a debriefing that focused on how the students felt about their experience.

Collins (1990) notes three problems in simply learning by doing: a *flexibility problem* (students learn to do things in only one way), a *learning problem* (students do not learn a global framework to organize their learning), and a *transfer problem* (students do not learn how to apply what they have learned in new situations). He proposes that, to construct robust understanding from situated experience, learners must articulate a global framework that can be used to integrate all the bits and pieces of knowledge gained from specific situations, reflect on situated experiences and relate them to the global framework, and explore and elaborate connections between situated experiences and the global framework. Influenced by Collins as well as Schön (1983), we have now redesigned the curricular structure of our program so that the initial problem enables the students to develop and articulate a global framework—the business concept.

We also implemented a rigorous assessment process that requires students to relate what they learn in any particular problem to their global framework—their understanding of the business concept. Finally, assessments may require them to address a similar situation, but in a different context. These assessments occur both while the students are addressing the problem—functioning as reflections-in-action—and after they have completed a problem, as reflections-after-action (Schön, 1983).

These changes have materially influenced our students' recognition of the breadth and depth of their own conceptual understanding, their ability to engage in nonassociated recall, and their skills in articulating their knowledge.

The Faculty as a Variable

In their review, Albanese and Mitchell (1993) largely ignored faculty attitude, capability, and orientation as variables that have an impact on problem-based learning. They noted only that the "role of facilitating discussion rather than directing it is foreign to many faculty" (p. 74). They also report some fragmentary research on faculty satisfaction with being a tutor. Our experience suggests that faculty are the central variable in effective implementation of problem-based learning.

Faculty Role. The role of the faculty member is quite different in problem-based learning from that in the traditional classroom. He or she spends very little time up front, lecturing and transferring information to students. Rather the role becomes a combination of both learning manager and coach.

The faculty selects appropriate learning problem-situations, a critical responsibility. The situations must be involving, relevant, holistic, and at the appropriate level of complexity. Further, the faculty must ensure that appropriate physical resources are present. This requirement ranges from arranging panels of executives who will review student presentations and provide feedback to ensuring that appropriate data resources are available at the library or via electronic sources.

But the teacher is also a coach (Kraft, 1988). The teacher observes, corrects, and encourages student performance. The coach-teacher "encourages that the right way of performing be done over and over again until the requisite skill becomes a firm and stable habit of performance" (Kraft, 1988, p. 1).

Much as happens in apprenticeship (Collins, Brown, and Newman, 1990), the teacher also provides a model. At appropriate times as students are involved in a learning situation, or after they have completed it, the teacher provides a thorough and high-quality performance so that students can compare their performance to that of an expert. This can be a personal performance demonstrated by the teacher or it can be a real-life or communicated performance by some other expert. Students need some involvement, some understanding of the context, before they can benefit from modeled performance.

Finally, the teacher helps students generalize the learning (Collins, Brown, and Newman, 1990). As students express (in oral or written form) what they have learned while confronting the problem-situation, the teacher helps them understand how that same knowledge and skill can be used in other situations. The transition to this richer faculty role can be extremely difficult for some faculty.

Faculty Orientation. Faculty members have been trained as experts in a narrow discipline to pass on their expertise to students and their professional colleagues. The models to which most have been exposed, primarily in their Ph.D. programs, have emphasized scholarly research. Teaching, to the extent it is addressed, emphasizes covering the content of the discipline through lecture and discussion. Little questioning is done regarding the relevance of the content to the practice of business or the effectiveness of the pedagogy in the preparation of students to become businesspeople.

Traditional faculty orientations are strongly embedded in the culture and in the profession and reinforced by the existing structures and reward systems. For most faculty members, the primary reference group comprises the leaders in their disciplinary field, not practicing businesspeople. While lip service is given to teaching, the reward system, including tenure and promotion, tends to emphasize publication of research articles in refereed, discipline-based journals.

Skills Required of Faculty

This new faculty role represents a paradigm shift calling for new skills. The paradigm shift has been expressed as moving from being the "sage on the stage" to serving as a "guide by the side." The basic skills required to be a "guide by the side" (active listening, coaching, mentoring, and facilitation) are not characteristic of a significant number of faculty members, and thus they must be learned. Once faculty members successfully navigate this paradigm shift—usually by starting to participate in problem-based learning and experiencing the *ah ha!*—most adjust by learning those new skills while developing new work habits.

Making the transition from the traditional faculty role to the richer role required in problem-based learning is not easy. It requires time, experimentation, nurturing, and support. Most central, however, is a willingness to move from a concern for teaching to a commitment to learning. This attitude shift moves faculty members from an input orientation to an outcomes orientation.

Will this transition become widespread? There is some hope. Reports such as the work of Porter and McKibbin (1988) reflect increased concern with preparing graduates to function effectively in business. Likewise, recent changes in American Assembly of Collegiate Schools of Business accreditation standards emphasize the move toward relevancy and outcomes-based education. But, to become more widespread, the transition will have to be championed by visionary leaders at the faculty and the administrative level. If the transition to establishing more meaningful learning communities is to continue, it will need to be reinforced by changing reward structures.

Student Transition

Students frequently express frustration when they first encounter problem-based learning. Most students have progressed through a typical educational system where knowledge is divided into arbitrary disciplines and taught to them through lectures, discussion sessions, or some combination. The students have learned to memorize information and regurgitate it on multiple choice, true-false, or essay examinations. This is a teacher-centered model of education, with the teacher and the textbook structuring all dimensions of learning.

Problem-based learning is student-centered. Students are expected to take responsibility for their own learning. The teacher does not tell them the "right answer." The teacher lets them experiment and make mistakes. The teacher makes them go to original sources to get information. The teacher may not even answer their questions directly. They are expected to find their own answers. This creates a very ambiguous situation for students.

"What are we supposed to do?"

"How do we do that?"

"If you would only tell me what you want, I would do it."

These are the types of statements we frequently hear. The situation is often most difficult for students who have been particularly strong performers in the positivist learning environment. They have functioned well where their life was structured for them, and perceive being forced to structure their own learning as very threatening.

Thus a great deal of coaching is required as students make the transition into problem-based learning. Students must be helped and encouraged as they start to take on responsibility for their own learning. Rather than just giving an assignment, the teacher must work with the students as they take their first halting steps into an ill-structured problem-situation. Rather than giving them a direct answer to a question, the teacher should talk them through the process of answering their own questions. If coached effectively through the transition, all but the most regimented of students make the transition and eventually thrive in the new learning environment.

Conclusion

We want to emphasize that we do not believe we have found the only right answers to the problem of how to best develop future business leaders. We have made serious entry into the arena of developing a genuine learning community. We are committed to continuing the search for better ways to assist students with learning. We believe this search will never end. When we begin to feel we are doing it right, it will be time to get out of the business.

References

Ackoff, R. "The Future of Operations Research Is Past." *Journal of Operations Research Society,* 1979, *30* (2), 93–104.

Albanese, M. A., and Mitchell, S. "Problem-Based Learning: A Review of Literature on Its Outcomes and Implementation Issues." *Academic Medicine,* 1993, *68* (1), 52–81.

Barrows, H. S. *How to Design a Problem-Based Curriculum for the Preclinical Years.* New York: Springer, 1985.

Brown, J. S., Collins, A., and Duguid, P. "Situated Cognition and the Culture of Learning." *Educational Researcher,* Jan.-Feb. 1989, pp. 89–99.

Business–Higher Education Forum. *America's Business Schools: Priorities for Change.* Report to the President, Washington, D.C., 1985.

Collins, A. "Generalizing from Situated Knowledge to Robust Understanding." Paper presented at the American Educational Research Association annual meeting, Boston, Apr. 1990.

Collins, A., Brown J., and Newman, S. "Cognitive Apprenticeship: Teaching the Craft of Reading, Writing, and Mathematics." In L. B. Resnick (ed.), *Cognition and Instruction: Issues and Agendas.* Hillsdale, N.J.: Erlbaum, 1990.

Duffy, T. M., and Jonassen, D. H. "Constructivism: New Implications for Instructional Technology." *Educational Technology,* 1991, *31* (5), 7–12.

Kraft, R. "Coaching to Learn." *The Teaching Professor,* 1988, 2 (1), 1–2.

Milter, R. G., and Stinson, J. E. "Educating Leaders for the New Competitive Environment." In W. H. Gijselaers, D. T. Tempelaar, P. K. Keizer, J. M. Blommaert, E. M. Bernard, and H. Kasper (eds.), *Educational Innovation in Economics and Business Administration: The Case of Problem-Based Learning.* Norwell, Mass.: Kluwer, 1995.

Porter, L., and McKibbin, L. *Management Education and Development: Drift or Thrust into the Twenty-First Century.* New York: McGraw-Hill, 1988.

Savery, J., and Duffy, T. "Problem-Based Learning: An Instructional Model and its Constructivist Framework." *Educational Technology,* Aug. 1994, 1–16.

Schank, R., and Cleary, C. *Engines for Education.* Technical Report no. 58. [http://www.ils.nwu.edu/~e_for_e/index.html]. 1995.

Schön, D. *The Reflective Practitioner.* New York: Basic Books, 1983.

Stinson, J. "Integrated Contextual Learning: Situated Learning in the Business Profession." Washington, D.C.: ERIC Clearinghouse on Higher Education, 1990. (ED 319330)

JOHN E. STINSON is professor of management in the College of Business at Ohio University, Athens, Ohio.

RICHARD G. MILTER is associate professor of management in the College of Business at Ohio University, Athens, Ohio.

In its use of complex, real-world problems to introduce concepts and motivate learning in an active and cooperative learning environment, problem-based learning provides a powerful alternative to the passive lecture tradition in introductory science courses in biology, physics, and chemistry.

The Power of Problem-Based Learning in Teaching Introductory Science Courses

Deborah E. Allen, Barbara J. Duch, Susan E. Groh

The past decade has seen a national call for change in both the *how* and the *what* of college science teaching (Czujko, 1994; Project Kaleidoscope, 1991; Tobias, 1990, 1992; Wingspread Conference, 1994). Traditionally, college science classes are taught using fifty-minute, content-driven lectures. Abstract concepts and principles are often presented first and only later illustrated with idealized examples that may be far removed from the students' personal experiences or interests. Memorization of facts and algorithmic problem solving are stressed, rather than conceptual understanding. The new information transferred to the student is assumed to fall into a preexisting framework with all the proper connections, automatically supplanting any contradictory ideas the student may already hold (Carey, 1986). Grade competition keeps students isolated; typical end-of-chapter, plug-and-chug exercises foster knowledge without conceptual understanding (Mazur, 1992).

In short, the structure of traditional science courses erects numerous roadblocks to students becoming actively involved in their own learning. Encouraging students to remain in this passive role in the classroom has the further unfortunate effects of promoting rote learning, obscuring the differences between high school and college thinking, and riveting intellectually immature students to a naive view of knowledge and its acquisition (Perry, 1968; Belenky, Clinchy, Goldberger, and Tarule, 1986; Magolda, 1992; Duch and Norton, 1992).

Note: This work has been partially supported by a grant from the National Science Foundation Program for Course and Curriculum Development.

We have a very different view of the science classroom. In answering the call that "science should be taught as science is practiced at its best" (American Association for the Advancement of Science, 1990, p. xi), we have designed several introductory science courses that use concrete, real-world problems to initiate the learning of new concepts through cooperative group efforts. Working together, students identify learning issues relevant to the problem, gather and share information that will address those issues, and respond to the challenge posed by the problem. In this integrated, problem-based approach to science instruction, the problems used to motivate and focus student learning also connect previous knowledge in science to new concepts to be mastered.

Why Problem-Based Learning?

Problem-based learning (PBL) addresses directly a number of the criticisms of current science education identified earlier.

Cooperative Small Groups. The use of cooperative working groups fosters the development of learning communities in science classes. Research has shown that student achievement is enhanced when students work together in a cooperative learning environment (Bodner, 1992; Johnson, Johnson, and Smith, 1991; Light, 1990). In addition, more women and minorities may be attracted to enter or stay in a science curriculum when the typical high competitiveness and isolation of science courses is removed (Tobias, 1990, 1992; Project Kaleidoscope, 1991). Working in groups also helps students develop essential characteristics necessary for success after graduation, such as verbal and written communication skills and team building skills (Czujko, 1994; Wingspread Conference, 1994).

Context. In PBL, students acquire scientific knowledge in the context in which it will be used. Students are more likely to retain what they learn and apply that knowledge appropriately when concepts are connected to applications (Coles, 1991; Dunkbase and Penick, 1990).

Learning to Learn. The scientific knowledge base is expanding exponentially, and students need to learn how to learn in the same manner that practicing scientists employ throughout their careers (Engel, 1991). Problem-based learning fosters the ability to identify what information is needed for a particular application, where and how to seek that information, how to organize it into a meaningful conceptual framework, and how to communicate the information so organized.

Doing Science. Problem-based learning provides an effective remedy for one of the most glaring problems in the traditional approach to teaching science; that is, the overwhelming tendency to proceed from the abstract to the concrete. By introducing an interesting, relevant problem up front, we capture students' attention and interest and allow them to experience for themselves the real process of doing science: they proceed from the known to the unknown, and in doing so can sense the origins of the abstract principles they later encounter.

Interdisciplinary Connections. The use of problems to introduce concepts also provides a natural mechanism to highlight the interconnections among disciplines. This approach strives to make obvious the underlying integration of scientific principles.

Models for Problem-Based Learning in Undergraduate Science Courses

Problem-based learning as a strategy for learning science has its roots in the medical school setting (Barrows and Tamblyn, 1980; Boud and Felleti, 1991), where intellectually mature and highly motivated students work in small groups with an assigned faculty tutor. This model is difficult to implement given the realities of the typical undergraduate educational setting, including class size and demands on faculty resources. At the University of Delaware, we have developed PBL models to address the needs of novice learners in small to medium-sized introductory courses in biology, chemistry, and physics. These models, while remaining centered on the analysis of problems by small groups of students, incorporate a greater degree of structure and support than the professional school PBL model. The next sections describe some of the characteristic features of our models.

Role of the Instructor. Empowering students to take an active, responsible role in the learning process requires faculty members to yield some of their authority in the classroom. The PBL instructor, whether in a medical school or an undergraduate setting, must trade at least a portion of this more traditional role for that of facilitator and activator of the students' learning initiatives. Working to guide, motivate, and probe the students' reasoning process as they journey through the problems rather than to direct it is often a less comfortable role, and requires a blend of creativity, ingenuity, and flexibility in its implementation (Mayo, Donnelly, and Schwartz, 1995; Wood, 1994).

Faculty members who serve as facilitators and activators for more than one PBL group or who teach relatively inexperienced learners, however, need to retain enough authority to ensure that the classroom events shaping the students' intellectual growth are carefully orchestrated. For introductory science orientation courses, an organizational scheme is critical in helping students develop a conceptual framework for the knowledge that they uncover. Without such a scheme, students may emerge from the course no better prepared to connect new knowledge to other applications or knowledge, or to distinguish the overriding principle from the trivial fact, than they would from a more traditional lecture course (Coles, 1991). On the other hand, this scheme must not unintentionally resurrect (in a new guise) the relatively secure stance of the traditional, more authoritative role, or allow the instructor to stage-manage the problem-solving process to the point of constraining the students' transition from passive to active learning.

Class Format. In problem-based learning, a crucial early step faced by each instructor is a decision, based on course objectives, student attitudes about the discipline, tutor availability, and a complex of other factors, as to the appropriate amount of class time to be spent on student-centered problem-solving activities. In the introductory biology course for freshman majors, a primary objective is to develop an active approach in understanding and using biological principles. In this course, group problem-solving is the principal activity, and the learning issues identified by the class and the results of the groups' investigations of those issues constitute the primary focus of discussion. In the physics course for sophomore and junior nonmajors, group problem-solving is again the principal activity, but is interspersed with lectures or whole-class discussions as needed to address more difficult issues. In the introductory chemistry course for freshman nonmajors, the need to deal with numerous abstract topics that are often difficult to approach adequately through problems is reflected in a format in which student-centered activities (group work on problem-solving and experiments) and teacher-centered activities (lectures, Socratic discussions, and demonstrations) are more evenly represented.

A distinct feature of our models is that while we do not lecture in advance on the particular learning issues students are likely to encounter in a given problem, neither do we present new problems to the class without introduction, as is commonplace in the traditional medical school PBL model (Engel, 1991; Blumberg and Michael, 1992). Rather, problems are introduced with minilectures that provide context and point out potential pitfalls and blind alleys likely to generate frustration. Likewise, we lead whole-class wrap-up sessions after each problem in which concepts that may still not be understood by some students or groups are explained either by the instructor or by a student volunteer and during which connections to past problems or to major principles are identified. Both the introductory minilectures and the wrap-up sessions provide opportunities for the instructors to model the problem-solving process for the students.

Groups. Students are assigned to a permanent working group of four to seven students, which functions as a unit for the length of the semester (fourteen weeks). Students may be assigned randomly or heterogeneously by major, year in college, or academic ability. Once formed, each group constructs its own ground rules. Typical ground rules deal with attendance policies, completing assigned work on schedule, ways of dealing with group assignments, and consequences for members who violate the rules. Equal participation is assured through roles such as discussion leader, recorder, reporter, and accuracy coach. In chemistry and physics, students rotate through these roles weekly, while in biology, the use of peer tutors (discussed later in this chapter) obviates the need for such roles.

Guiding Students Through the Problems. We have developed several strategies by which a single instructor can effectively guide one or more groups through problems. All strategies require problems with natural break points at which the instructor may easily intervene without intruding upon student initiatives. These planned points of intervention always provide a compelling reason, such as a critical piece of information, for students to shift their focus from group activities to the instructor. During these breaks, whole-class discussions led by the instructor are used to clarify common misconceptions, introduce the next stage of the problem, or encourage groups to compare notes on their progress. Between these breaks, the instructor rotates among the groups, ideally spending five to ten minutes with each to prevent overengagement in one group's activities to the exclusion of others who may be having difficulties. If common roadblocks are perceived, the class is brought back together spontaneously to receive pointers and clarifications. In this "floating facilitator" model, optimal group functioning is aided by small group size and role assignments.

Another model we developed uses upperclass undergraduate peer tutors to guide students through problems during the class period. This model is particularly well suited for courses with too many groups for a single facilitator to monitor in one class period, or in which an objective is to have introductory students unravel complex problems in subject areas not commonly tackled at this level. Experience to date from introductory biology is that these peer tutors, when coached and supported by the course instructor, can be as competent at facilitating tutorial groups as faculty. A similar conclusion was reached in a study (Moust and Schmidt, 1992) of the efficacy of peer tutors in facilitating the learning of first-year law students at the University of Limburg. Peer tutors provide additional advantages in that they operate at a conceptual level closer to that of the students than does the instructor. They also represent a less threatening instructor role, allowing students to more freely acknowledge what they do not know. This model does not exempt the course instructor from the "floating facilitator" role, but typically lessens the necessity for bringing the class together for clarification.

The Problems. A crucial component of PBL is the introduction of concepts and principles through the use of problems. Good problems share a number of characteristic features:

- They tell engaging stories in settings to which the students can relate, thus solidifying the eventual connection between theory and application.
- They are open-ended, challenging students to make and justify estimations and assumptions.
- They engender controversy or require decisions, so their solutions require students to demonstrate thinking skills beyond simple knowledge and comprehension.
- They are complex enough for students in each group to recognize the need to work together to succeed in arriving at a satisfactory conclusion.

Since the use of problem-based learning in introductory science courses is a new development, there exists as yet no handy compilation of tried and tested problems for the interested instructor. The traditional end-of-chapter exercises found in most texts are narrowly focused on the chapter topic, and many times encourage students to pattern-match or plug and chug in search of *the* correct answer. Nonetheless, these can often serve as the foundation for rich, complex problems that go several levels beyond the original. For example, in physics the concepts implicit in a simple exercise concerning electrical currents in parallel circuits were transformed into a more elaborate problem in which the students must design a safe electrical system for a house, based on the number and type of circuits available, the appliances to be used, patterns of usage, and so on. The underlying physics concepts are the same in both the exercise and the problem, but the latter provides a much greater opportunity for enriched, higher-level learning. Texts also often provide final "essay boxes" that describe some practical or interesting application of the concepts discussed in each chapter. These applications can be used to introduce the same concepts, engaging the students' interest up front and providing a motive for learning.

As it should, the real world provides a wealth of ideas for problems. Newspapers, magazines, radio, television, and cinema serve as very useful sources, as do observations of the natural phenomena of daily life. Articles from the primary scientific literature can also be important sources. We have found that using problem-based learning has made us, as instructors, much more aware of our learning objectives, with respect to both content and pedagogy issues. Many of our best problems stem from a triggering article or incident that captures our imaginations as we recognize within it elements appropriate to those objectives.

Learning Resources. As one of our goals is to promote student-centered learning, the instructors do not supply students with all the information that they need to solve a problem; rather, students are encouraged to explore a variety of resources in seeking the information they require. These may include textbooks, supplementary materials specified by the instructor, general library reference sources, including the Internet and World Wide Web, other students, and other faculty. The emphasis varies from course to course. In biology, students make significant use of the library in researching their learning issues. Early in the semester, the class is given a tour of the library and shown where to find and how to use the most relevant literature. In physics and chemistry, the textbooks serve as primary sources of information, although specific reading assignments are not generally given. Students learn that the information they need may be found anywhere in the text, not just in the current chapter. Students are also encouraged to consider other faculty members and classmates as resources, just as they would in solving a problem in the real world.

Assessment. As is often pointed out (Wood, 1994; Ory and Ryan, 1993), exams drive student learning, even in a PBL course. Thus for the PBL instructor whose objectives include acquisition of skills as well as content knowledge, methods for assessing competency in "what students can *do* as well as what they can remember" (Wood, 1994, p. 81) assume critical importance. Our assessments include: group projects requiring extensive out-of-class research and collaborative effort; hour exams that use problems requiring students to reapply concepts previously used in solving in-class problems; and the *triple-jump exam* developed by faculty at McMaster University (Painvin and others,

1979). In the triple-jump exam, students are given a problem to analyze and a fixed amount of study time to resolve self-identified learning issues. The exam ends with individual oral examinations based on what they have learned. In introductory biology, an option offered in place of the final exam was the preparation of a short paper (five to six pages) updating some aspect of a problem encountered during the semester, using a combination of original research papers, articles from the popular science press, and review articles.

Peer Evaluation. In a cooperative learning environment in which assessment is based even partially on group products, students need to feel that they have some control over the behavior of their peers before they are confident enough to enter into the group efforts wholeheartedly (Johnson, Johnson, and Smith, 1991). Instituting a system of peer evaluation helps to provide this sense of control. All three of our courses use similar evaluation schemes in which students are asked several times during the course to rate the members of their group and themselves according to several criteria. These include: attendance, degree of preparation for class, listening and communication skills, ability to bring new and relevant information to the group, ability to ask questions that further group understanding, and ability to support and improve the functioning of the group as a whole. The ratings are based on a numerical scale and the resulting values constitute part (up to ten percent) of the student's overall course grade. When peer tutors are used, their ratings of their students' group skills also enter into the overall evaluation. The tutor's rating of an individual is equal in weight to the collective rating of the other group members.

Student Reaction to PBL

Student responses to various aspects of these courses on final course rating forms and in interviews with an independent consultant have been consistently positive. In general, students in all three courses indicated that they felt comfortable working in groups and that working in groups aided their learning.

"Group work helped me see there's more than one way to approach a problem."
"Combined knowledge makes it easier to solve problems."
"Teaching others in the group has made me think critically and analytically."
"Group work made learning more fun."

Perhaps not surprisingly, though, the degree to which students perceive group work as contributing positively to their learning reflects the emphasis in both time and grading given it in the course. Students in the biology and physics courses, in which group activities dominated and in which there were significant group components to grades, felt that group work was very beneficial, giving this item a mean rating of 1.1 on a scale rating effects on learning of 1 (very beneficial) to 5 (very detrimental). In the chemistry course, in which group work did not receive the same degree of emphasis, its beneficial effects were seen to be less substantial (mean rating of 2.6). It may be that to reap the maximum learning benefit from group work, such activities need to play a principal role in the course format.

Students also related that the use of real-world problems was beneficial to their learning, and that after their experiences in working on these complex problems, they felt confident in their ability to apply basic principles to solve other problems.

"They [the problems] helped unite the concepts."
"They're like a mystery that needed to be figured out—so you wanted to finish it."
"I learned a lot—[the problems] applied to me and my body, which made it interesting."
"[The problems] seemed to incorporate so many things. They were relevant and timely."

While all three classes found such problems beneficial, the perception of these benefits was more obvious in the biology and physics courses, again reflecting, presumably, the central role played by the problems in these courses.

The Future of PBL in Undergraduate Science Courses

Problem-based learning has captured the interest of a growing number of faculty members at the University of Delaware in fields as diverse as geology, agricultural biotechnology, and nutrition, as well as the traditional science fields of biology, chemistry, and physics. These faculty members are developing models that will extend PBL into undergraduate science beyond the basic practices we have adopted for our small to medium-sized introductory courses. Of particular interest are the use of technology and multimedia as the basis for problems, the development of models for large classes, and the use of interdisciplinary problems to promote science literacy among nonmajors. Incorporating problems as an integral part of laboratory classes is proving to be an effective way of using PBL with the large-enrollment science courses. These collective efforts on the part of a critical mass of science faculty members will allow us, in the future, to evaluate the effectiveness of this method of science instruction in a variety of settings.

What Is the Power of Problem-Based Learning?

Using PBL, we have found that students are active, participating and questioning throughout class. They continually challenge us with questions that go well beyond the basic principles normally addressed in introductory courses. Would we return to lecturing in a traditional fashion? Not a chance! The excitement and energy of a roomful of students working in groups, teaching each other, challenging each other, and questioning each other is what we value in our classrooms.

What is the power of problem-based learning? We agree with Goode-nough (1991, p. 98) that the power of PBL "has nothing to do with self-aggran-dizement or adulation by students and peers. Rather, it is the power of meaningful interconnection among students and teachers as they all learn and, in a very real sense, transcend themselves, adding a vital new layer to the grow-ing coral reef of human understanding."

References

American Association for the Advancement of Science. "The Liberal Art of Science: Agenda for Action." In *Report of the Project on Liberal Education and the Sciences*. Washington, D.C.: American Association for the Advancement of Science, 1990.

Barrows, H. S., and Tamblyn, R. N. *Problem-Based Learning: An Approach to Medical Education*. New York: Springer, 1980.

Belenky, M. F., Clinchy, B. M., Goldberger, N. R., and Tarule, J. M. *Women's Ways of Knowing: The Development of Self, Voice, and Mind*. New York: Basic Books, 1986.

Blumberg, P., and Michael, J. A. "Development of Self-Directed Learning Behaviors in a Partially Teacher-Directed Problem-Based Learning Curriculum." *Teaching and Learning in Medicine*, 1992, 4 (1), 3–8.

Bodner, G. M. "Why Changing the Curriculum May Not be Enough." *Journal of Chemical Education*, 1992, 69, 186–190.

Boud, D., and Felleti, G. "Introduction." In D. Boud and G. Felle ti (eds.), *The Challenge of Problem-Based Learning*. New York: St. Martin's Press, 1991.

Carey, S. "Cognitive Science and Science Education." *American Psychologist*, 1986, 41 (10), 1123–1130.

Coles, C. "Is Problem-Based Learning the Only Way?" In D. Boud and G. Feletti (eds.), *The Challenge of Problem-Based Learning*. New York: St. Martin's Press, 1991.

Czujko, R. "Physics Job Market: A Statistical Overview." *AAPT Announcer*, 1994, 24 (4), 62.

Duch, B. J., and Norton, M. "Teaching for Cognitive Growth." *Teaching Excellence: Toward the Best in the Academy*, a publication of the Professional and Organizational Development Network in Higher Education, 1992, 4 (8), 1–2.

Dunkbase, J. A., and Penick, E. "Problem Solving in the Real World." *Journal of College Science Teaching*, 1990, 19 (6), 367–370.

Engel, J. "Not Just a Method But a Way of Learning." In D. J. Boud and G. Feletti (eds.), *The Challenge of Problem-Based Learning*. New York: St. Martin's Press, 1991.

Goodenough, D. A. "Changing Ground: Medical School Lecturer Turns to Discussion Teaching." In C. R. Christensen, D. A. Garvin, and A. Sweet (eds.), *Education for Judgment: The Artistry of Discussion Leadership*. Boston: Harvard Business School, 1991.

Johnson, D. W., Johnson, R. T., and Smith, K. A. *Cooperative Learning: Increasing College Faculty Instructional Productivity*. ASHE-ERIC Higher Education Report No. 4. Washington, D.C.: School of Education and Human Development, George Washington University, 1991.

Light, R. J. *The Harvard Assessment Seminars*. Cambridge, Mass.: Harvard University Press, 1990.

Magolda, M.B.B. *Knowing and Reasoning in College: Gender-Related in Students' Intellectual Development*. San Francisco: Jossey-Bass, 1992.

Mayo, W. P., Donnelly, M. B., and Schwartz, R. W. "Characteristics of the Ideal Problem-Based Learning Tutor in Clinical Medicine." *Evaluation and the Health Professions*, 1995, 18 (2), 124–136.

Mazur, E. "Qualitative vs. Quantitative Thinking: Are We Teaching the Right Thing?" *Optics and Phonics News*, Feb. 1992, p. 38.

Moust, J. C., and Schmidt, H. G. "Undergraduate Students as Tutors: Are They as Effective as Faculty in Conducting Small-Group Tutorials?" Paper presented at the annual meeting of the American Educational Research Association, San Francisco, Apr. 1992.

Ory, J. C., and Ryan, K. E. *Tips for Improving Testing and Grading.* Thousand Oaks, Calif.: Sage, 1993.

Painvin, C., Neufeld, V. R., Norman, G. R., Walker, I., and Whelan, G. "The *Triple Jump Exercise*—A Structured Measure of Problem-Solving and Self-Directed Learning." *Research in Medical Education Proceedings of the Eighteenth Annual Conference,* 1979, 23, 73–77.

Perry, W. *Forms of Intellectual and Ethical Growth in the College Years.* Austin, Tex.: Holt, Rinehart and Winston, 1968.

Project Kaleidoscope. *What Works: Building Natural Science Communities,* Vol. 1. Washington, D.C.: Stamats Communications, 1991.

Tobias, S. *They're Not Dumb, They're Different.* Tucson, Ariz.: Research Corporation, 1990.

Tobias, S. *Revitalizing Undergraduate Science.* Tucson, Ariz.: Research Corporation, 1992.

Wingspread Conference. "Quality Assurance in Undergraduate Education: What the Public Expects." Denver, Colo.: Education Commission of the States, 1994.

Wood, E. J. "The Problems of Problem-Based Learning." *Biochemical Education,* 1994, 22 (2), 78–82.

DEBORAH E. ALLEN *is assistant professor of biology at the University of Delaware.*

BARBARA J. DUCH *is a teaching consultant in the Center for Teaching Effectiveness and a physics instructor at the University of Delaware.*

SUSAN E. GROH *is assistant professor of chemistry and biochemistry in the university honors program at the University of Delaware.*

*Problem-based learning has been used to address acknowledged
shortcomings in leadership education. This innovative approach
required changes in the nature of the learning materials, classroom
process, instructor's role, and student assessment procedures.*

Problem-Based Learning
in Leadership Education

Edwin M. Bridges, Philip Hallinger

Seven years ago, we introduced problem-based learning (PBL) to educational
administration through a master's degree program for prospective public school
principals at the Stanford University School of Education. Since then, this
approach has been used in many different formats and contexts ranging in size
from 6 to 150 participants—week-long institutes, two- and three-day staff
development workshops, semester courses for part-time students meeting on
weekends, quarter-long courses for full-time students, and distance learning.
The students have been professors of educational administration, undergraduates, graduate students, and practicing administrators within and outside the
field of education. More recently, professors and staff developers have used our
approach in Thailand and Australia to prepare school leaders, hotel managers,
and medical school administrators.

Our initial interest in PBL stemmed from concerns about the character of
existing leadership education programs, including our own. Most programs
view their purpose as imparting knowledge and honing the mode of analytic
thinking prized in institutions of higher education. Students learn about leadership in the abstract and, to a more limited extent, how to use this information to analyze situations that may bear little similarity to professional practice.
They learn almost nothing about the types of problems they will encounter as
leaders; they do not learn to apply knowledge to these problems; they do not
develop skill in running meetings and writing effective memos; and they
acquire little insight into the emotional aspects of leadership.

Note: The authors wish to acknowledge the valuable comments of William R. Mulford on
an earlier draft of this chapter.

Moreover, the education students receive occurs within a classroom setting that bears little resemblance to the context in which leaders perform their roles (Bridges, 1977). In traditional leadership programs, students occupy a passive, individualistic, subordinate role rather than an active, interdependent, superordinate role. They learn to write using academic forms of communication rather than those more characteristic of managerial work, such as memos. Students also learn in an emotional climate much more placid and neutral than the one leaders face. Finally, the relatively slow tempo of the student's classroom role contrasts sharply with the accelerated work pace of an administrator. With this kind of preparation, graduates of these programs experience reality shock when they start working as leaders; they feel ill-prepared to deal with the emotional and cognitive demands of the role and often suffer from what has been called *analysis paralysis.*

As we contemplated the deficiencies of current programs in leadership education and learned more about PBL, we became convinced that PBL had the potential to address most, if not all, of these shortcomings. In this chapter, we discuss the version of PBL that we created to overcome these widely acknowledged limitations of leadership education (Bridges, 1977; Griffiths, Stout, and Forsyth, 1988; Murphy, 1992).

Choice of Method

According to Barrows (1986), one should decide on major educational objectives and then select the method of learning that best fits these objectives. The version of PBL that we have designed reflects our belief that *the essence of leadership is getting results through others.* Our main objectives derive from this belief and emphasize the following skills: facilitating group problem solving, building consensus, communicating ideas, acquiring the knowledge needed to deal with problems facing school leaders, implementing solutions to these problems, and dealing with the emotional aspects of leadership.

To accomplish these objectives, we have structured the basic unit of instruction around a problem-based learning project. Much of a leader's work occurs in the context of temporary projects created to accomplish a limited set of objectives under time constraints using available resources. By conceiving of the PBL module as a project, we create a learning context that mirrors the work environment. Learning is motivated by confronting a complex problem that requires active engagement and resolution in the form of a product. Resolution is bounded in terms of time, and the problem is addressed in collaboration with others.

One consequence of the project-based approach is that it forces students to cope with the emotional, as well as the cognitive, demands of leadership. The projects provide opportunities for students to test their competence in interpreting and responding to the feelings of others. Moreover, while working on the projects, the team members often find themselves struggling with the dilemma that confronts every conscientious leader, how to achieve a high level of performance and sustain group cohesiveness within severe time constraints. This dilemma requires students to make difficult choices, to set priorities, and to experience the consequences.

Each PBL project typically takes three to five classes to complete, with each class lasting approximately three hours. However, students often become so engaged with the project that they meet longer and more frequently than required.

Learning Materials

Each project centers around learning materials consisting of four components: the focal problem, the content, the culminating product or performance, and the learning objectives. In our recent book on PBL, we discuss these components more fully and describe the process for creating these projects (Bridges and Hallinger, 1995).

The Problem. The focal problem is a typically messy situation that students are likely to encounter in their future professional practice. It may also be a problem that affects large numbers of people for an extended period of time. The problem drives choices about learning objectives, content, and the product or performance. Focal problems include the transition of a public school from an English-speaking student body to one consisting of native English, limited-English-proficient, and non-English-proficient students; a breakdown in school discipline; a school with a veteran faculty, a changing student population, and declining test scores; and a problem teacher who has tenure, to name only a few.

We present these problems in different formats. Several appear in the form of highly contextualized written cases; others are introduced via videotape, computer simulations, or live simulations.

For example, the *Safety and Order* project contains a written case that centers around a high school with a growing gang problem and a history of student violence. While working on this problem, students experience four unannounced interruptions, three portrayed by trained models. The first interruption involves a conference with a 10th-grade male student referred to the office. The students, in the role of the principal, have only twenty minutes to learn why the student has been referred and to decide what to do. If the student principals ask the right questions, they learn that the student, although possessing a spotless citizenship record and high grades, has struck and injured another student during physical education class. The second interruption is a conference with the parent of the offending student. The parent believes that the penalty is too severe and demands that his son receive only a reprimand. The third interruption involves an interview with a newspaper reporter about a letter to the editor from the aggrieved parent and discipline at the school. A subsequent, negatively slanted newspaper article by the reporter provides the fourth interruption.

This combination of factually presented material and live surprises models several characteristics of on-the-job practice: unpredictability, ambiguity, and working on several problems at once.

Content. The content for each project is drawn from relevant disciplines and craft knowledge or practical wisdom. Students encounter this content through a variety of means—readings, instructional tapes, videotaped reflections of scholars and practitioners on the problem, and consultations with experts. This content illuminates aspects of the problem and its resolution. For example, as students work through the problem of a school undergoing change in the language proficiency of its students, they learn about the legal aspects of serving a multilingual student population, theory and research on second-language acquisition, how public schools have treated recent immigrants, examples of school bilingual programs and district policies, and research on newcomer centers.

This multidisciplinary approach mirrors the way knowledge application occurs in the workplace. The important problems that leaders face on the job tend to be multifaceted and to require the use of knowledge from several domains.

Product. Every PBL project includes a performance product. This product engages students in developing a solution to the problem(s) and in presenting that solution via the same mode used in the workplace. The mode of resolution varies with the nature of the problem and might include a presentation, a conference, an agenda and supporting material for the first meeting of a task force, a strategic plan, or a memo. Guidelines for creating these performance products are ambiguous so that students become accustomed to dealing with unclear tasks and the attendant psychological discomfort.

The products also force students to grapple with issues inherent in getting results through others. Students must confront varying views about what the problem is and how it should be handled. In addition, they need to decide how they should organize themselves to create the product within the time constraints. These products also provide an incentive for learning and a way for them to judge the effectiveness of their collective efforts.

The impact of the performance product in this model of PBL has surprised us. Being responsible for a performance product provides a sharper focus to the problem solving in which students engage. The performance product component of the PBL project moves it beyond an abstract exercise, and students typically exhibit the performance anxiety one would anticipate in a real, not a contrived, setting. While this is particularly critical for the learning of novice leaders, it is also an important motivational and practical tool for engaging veteran leaders.

Learning Objectives. The learning objectives provided at the outset of each project accent what students will learn from it. These objectives relate to the problem-relevant knowledge that is the project focus, as well as the knowledge and skills needed to complete the product. For example, in the project that centers on a school undergoing a major change in the linguistic and cultural composition of its student body, we identified managing an advisory committee or task force as a major requisite skill. Suspecting that students lacked this skill, we incorporated it into the objectives along with such problem-relevant goals as knowledge of the theory and research on second-language acquisition. Although we generally suggest five to seven learning objectives per project, we have found it productive for students to personalize their learning by focusing on those objectives that pertain to gaps in their own professional background.

Classroom Process

Our version of PBL differs in two major respects from PBL as described by Barrows and Tamblyn (1980) and Schmidt (1983). First, we have substantially altered the role of facilitator; second, we have placed considerable emphasis on implementation.

In the small group tutorial format of PBL, the instructor or an advanced graduate student remains an active facilitator in the group's learning process but does not provide direct instruction. In problem-based leadership education, students work without the active facilitation of a tutor and manage virtually the entire process for the duration of each project. This format creates the opportunity for students to learn and practice skills essential to getting results through people, namely, managing projects, running meetings, resolving conflict, building consensus, and collaborating with others to define problems and reach decisions.

Our model of PBL also attaches much greater weight to implementing decisions than is the case in more typical approaches. Since implementation skills are essential to effective leadership, we explicitly incorporate action-oriented performances into the projects so that students can experience in a limited fashion the consequences of their actions. By according coequal status to problem analysis and implementation, we strive to prepare students who will not suffer from the kind of analysis paralysis attributed to other programs.

During each project, students are assigned to a team of six to seven members. Class sessions are treated as meetings of the project team. During these meetings, students play the roles of leader, facilitator, recorder, or group member. The student acting as the leader functions in that capacity for the entire project. Leaders have primary responsibility for organizing the project to accomplish the objectives and to complete the product. They create a tentative completion plan for the time allotted and play a major role in drafting each session's agenda, including what the team tries to accomplish during the session and how it plans to proceed.

Other members of the project team take turns acting as facilitators or recorders. The facilitator suggests processes for dealing with each item on the agenda, keeps the group on task, and assists the group in reaching agreement on problem definition and resolution actions. The recorder records major ideas and decisions, and prepares a written record of the group's work.

Most projects culminate with the students' actually implementing their response in the form of a realistic product or performance. Implementation forces them to struggle with a range of political, cultural, organizational, and human issues inherent in putting action plans into effect. In addition, they become aware of the need to anticipate potential problems, assess their seriousness, and develop preventive or contingency plans for the most serious potential problems. Students also confront the realistic possibility that their solution may not work. If things go poorly, they learn how to deal constructively with frustration and disappointment. If things go well, the students' level of confidence in their ability increases.

By way of illustration, in one project the team is the committee responsible for designing and implementing a teacher selection process (Bridges with Hallinger, 1992). The committee then implements the process with three finalists. The team evaluates how well each finalist has performed during the selection process and prepares a one-page memo to the director of personnel. The memo describes the vacancy and the process used, recommends one of the three finalists (if that seems appropriate), and justifies its recommendation. The selection process includes an interview and an observation of each finalist teaching a group of students like those the teacher will teach.

Given the emphasis placed on the product and its implementation, students may become so preoccupied with solving the problem and creating the product that they slight the learning objectives. As a response to this potential difficulty, the leader has the responsibility of ensuring that the learning objectives, as well as the product, are accomplished. If leaders sense that the team is cutting corners to get the product out the door, they act as the group's conscience and refocus them on the learning objectives. Their success as leaders depends in part on how well they manage the tension between completing the product and accomplishing the learning objectives.

Role of the Instructor

When discussing the role of the instructor in this version of PBL, it is useful to distinguish between the faculty attitudes crucial to success in a PBL environment and faculty actions prior to, during, and following a PBL project (Bridges and Hallinger, 1995).

Faculty Attitudes. Our version of PBL tests both the patience and confidence of instructors. A PBL project seldom runs smoothly. Students typically experience considerable confusion mixed with a measure of nervousness about the approach of the professor and the ambiguity of the situation. They may become frustrated and direct their hostility toward the instructor. We believe that instructors must maintain a vantage point above the affective and cognitive turmoil that students experience. They "need to preserve the perspective that for students being *lost at sea* is part of the journey; not far off, near the horizon, are calmer waters that lead toward the desired destination" (Bridges and Hallinger, 1995, p. 54). Without this perspective, instructors may actually feed the students' anxiety or may take a more active role, thus undermining the self-directed learning process.

Easing the Transition. Instructors can facilitate the transition to PBL and reduce frustration in various ways. To inform students about PBL and build their confidence in the approach, instructors can use a PBL project such as the one we have developed for this purpose, "Because Wisdom Cannot be Told" (in Bridges and Hallinger, 1995). The process and the content of this project work together to foster understanding of and appreciation for problem-based learning. Instructors can also ease the transition by gradually increasing the complexity of the projects. Finally, instructors can promote student success by having students learn skills in project and meeting management, problem solving, consensus building, memo writing, and oral presentation. By introducing these skills early in a leadership curriculum, the instructor provides students repeated opportunities to practice and refine these skills. Dumping students into PBL without attending to this transition may lead to disastrous results.

Front-Loading Effort. In our experience and that of other users, our version of PBL requires considerably more time and attention initially than instructors are accustomed to in conventional courses (Chenoweth and Everhart, 1994). Front-loading takes several forms: creating or selecting the learning materials, reviewing and preparing PBL project materials for student use, and attending to the numerous logistical details—for example, preparing the physical environment, assigning students to teams and roles, identifying consultants, and providing equipment. Inadequate advance attention to these issues decreases the efficiency and effectiveness of students' learning.

Developing Classroom Norms. To facilitate learning in a PBL leadership environment, it is important to develop several classroom norms. One of the most important norms relates to how mistakes are viewed. Instructors should establish an environment in which mistakes are learning opportunities. There are few safe havens for leaders and prospective leaders to acquire new skills and knowledge and to practice using them without fear of unleashing irreversible consequences. In our PBL courses, the greatest learning has occurred when students experience something akin to failure and reflect on how and why that happened. This, however, places a much greater premium on providing constructive feedback. Other norms relate to time use, developing a problem-focused orientation to learning, personalizing learning, resourceful learning, and self-monitoring (Bridges and Hallinger, 1995).

Interacting with Students. During a PBL project, the instructor lives in the background almost all of the time. The instructor acts primarily as a process observer during meetings of the project team, clarifies project-specific issues that arise, consults on individual matters, monitors and modifies the time allocated for completion, and conducts regular debriefings.

Evaluation of Students

Like so many users of problem-based learning, we have grappled with the issue of evaluation. Fully cognizant of the lack of consensus about this topic, we adopted several principles to guide the forms evaluation would take. First, to promote transfer of learning, we base evaluation on the performance of tasks similar to the ones performed by school leaders, not on mere recall and comprehension of knowledge. Second, to promote student growth, we devote our attention to providing feedback that details each student's strengths and areas in need of improvement instead of summary ratings of performance. Finally, to cultivate habits of self-evaluation and reflection, we have students assess the quality of their own performance.

With these guiding principles in mind, we have experimented with a wide variety of tools and techniques for assessment, such as:

- Integrative essays in which students discuss what they have learned during a project and how they might use the knowledge and skills in the future
- Protocols or standards that students may use to evaluate their own performance or products
- Models or examples of products completed by expert practitioners against which to compare their own products
- Knowledge-review exercises that test the students' ability to apply their knowledge to typical situations
- Forms created by students to elicit feedback from their peers on aspects of their performance
- Structured observations that provide descriptive information about individual and group performance
- Probing questions for students to consider in relation to their final performance products

Numerous examples of these assessment tools and techniques appear in Bridges and Hallinger (1995).

Conclusion

Since this version of PBL is a newcomer to the field of leadership education, there has been limited evaluation of its effectiveness. In the one program (Stanford) that has used this instructional approach most extensively and for the longest period, the results are encouraging.

In the spring of 1995, the newly appointed dean of the Stanford School of Education commissioned a comprehensive internal and external review of its academic programs. The Prospective Principals Program was the only one singled out for special accolades. All graduates who were interviewed mentioned the problem-based orientation of the program as a basis for its excellence. When asked to comment on the appropriateness of the emphasis placed on PBL in curriculum (roughly 40 percent), students consistently answered, "Don't alter the emphasis. It is too intense to be increased and too valuable to be reduced." Admittedly, these results provide a limited basis for evaluation. At the same time, they coincide with our personal assessments of problem-based learning. Our experience with PBL suggests that it can address certain intractable problems encountered in the professional education of both future and practicing leaders.

References

Barrows, H. S. "A Taxonomy of Problem-Based Learning Methods." *Medical Education,* 1986, 20, 481–486.

Barrows, H. S., and Tamblyn, R. N. *Problem-Based Learning: An Approach to Medical Education.* New York: Springer, 1980.

Bridges, E. M. "The Nature of Leadership." In L. Cunningham, W. Hack, and R. Nystrand (eds.), *Educational Administration: The Developing Decades.* Berkeley, Calif.: McCutchan, 1977.

Bridges, E. M., with Hallinger, P. *Problem Based Learning for Administrators.* Eugene, Ore.: ERIC Clearinghouse on Educational Management, 1992.

Bridges, E. M., and Hallinger, P. *Implementing Problem Based Learning in Leadership Development.* Eugene, Ore.: ERIC Clearinghouse on Educational Management, 1995.

Chenoweth, T., and Everhart, R. "Preparing Leaders to Understand and Facilitate Change: A Problem-Based Learning Approach." *Journal of School Leadership,* 1994, 4 (4), 414–431.

Griffiths, D., Stout, R., and Forsyth, P. "The Preparation of Educational Administrators." In D. Griffiths, R. Stout, and P. Forsyth (eds.), *Leaders for America's Schools.* Berkeley, Calif.: McCutchan, 1988.

Murphy, J. *The Landscape of Leadership Preparation.* Thousand Oaks, Calif.: Corwin Press, 1992.

Schmidt, H. G. "Problem-Based Learning: Rationale and Description." *Medical Education,* 1983, 17, 11–16.

EDWIN M. BRIDGES *is professor of education and director of the Prospective Principals Program, Stanford University School of Education.*

PHILIP HALLINGER *is professor of educational leadership at Vanderbilt University and at the Center for Leadership Development, Chiang Mai University, Thailand.*

An inquiry course in an interdisciplinary program is described. The essence of problem-based learning is preserved though the class is three times the size of a normal tutorial group.

Twenty-Up: Problem-Based Learning with a Large Group

P. K. Rangachari

The tacit aim of all educational enterprises is the production of confident, self-reliant, reflective students who can comfortably ignore the presence of the teacher (Rangachari, 1995). Achieving this is easier hoped for than reached, however (Boud, 1988). Problem-based learning (PBL) has the potential to encourage active learning, a necessary step in that direction. The small group, self-directed tutorial format has become the most common expression for PBL and has been used in a variety of professional programs (Albanese and Mitchell, 1993; Boud and Felleti, 1991).

In 1989, I was asked to teach an inquiry course for upper division undergraduates enrolled in the arts and sciences program at McMaster University. This is an interdisciplinary program that offers students an opportunity "to use their university years to further their intellectual growth through a study of significant achievements in both arts and sciences and of the methods of inquiry." The program has a limited enrollment and has usually attracted highly motivated students with far above average high school grades. The core curriculum is designed to give students an understanding of the sciences, technology, and the arts, and to help them develop skills in oral and written language and quantitative reasoning. It fosters skills for practical inquiry into problems of public concern through a series of courses.

To maintain the spirit of inquiry I sought to design a course to help students explore issues related to health and illness in the modern world. PBL

Note: A special debt of gratitude to the students who took this course; sincere thanks to the directors of the arts and sciences program (Herbert Jenkins and Barbara Ferrier) and to Kathy Ryan and J. Miller in the administration for their help; also to McMaster University, which still believes that teaching is part of its mandate.

appeared to be an excellent format for the course, and I initially proposed a conventional small group tutorial course modeled on the undergraduate M.D. program at this university. However, when eighteen students enrolled I was forced to reconsider my options. I decided to reflect carefully on what the essence of problem-based learning was and to modify my course to suit the larger number of students.

The resulting course (The Curing Society) has been in operation since that time. Although several changes have been incorporated, the format has been preserved. This essay describes the current version of that course, concentrating particularly on the differences between the format used and the conventional small group tutorial model of PBL.

Problem-Based Learning: The Cardinal Elements

The term problem-based learning means different things to different people (Barrows and Tamblyn, 1980). Shorn of all rhetoric, it is a format that encourages active participation by plunging students into a situation requiring them to define their own learning needs within broad goals set by the faculty. The students are presented with problem-situations that serve as springboards for learning. This is in sharp contrast to subject-based approaches that teach a body of knowledge prior to its application to specific problems.

In the traditional variant of PBL (Branda, 1990), students meet in small groups and use a variety of stimuli, such as paper problems, real cases, and videotapes, to generate issues that are refined into learning tasks. They then seek, synthesize, and integrate information about these tasks, which they share with each other in subsequent sessions. This self-directed learning requires continuous evaluation and monitoring of progress, which is carried out in the tutorials.

For my course, I have extracted what I believe are the cardinal elements of problem-based learning. These are the provision of problem-situations as starting points for inquiry, the framing of learning tasks to guide the search, synthesis, and integration of information by the students, and the subsequent sharing of that information with the group. An integral component of the process is the participation of the students in the evaluative process.

In problem-based courses, process and content are inextricably linked. Process refers to how something is learned whereas content refers to what is learned. The five components just listed constitute the process objectives for my course, as for all problem-based courses.

The content or *what* of any course has two distinct elements or components. (To avoid semantic confusion, I prefer to use the words components or elements rather than objectives.) These can be either instructional or expressive (Eisner, 1985). The instructional components are the items of information that the student is expected to either acquire or demonstrate a familiarity with. Expressive components are more problematic. Rather than specifying items of information, an expressive component merely suggests an educational encounter that provides an opportunity to explore, defer, or focus on issues that appear to be of particular interest. They are thus "evocative rather than prescriptive" (Eisner, 1985, p. 55). All courses have both components, but an upper-level inquiry course should stress expressive rather than instructional components.

For my specific course, the instructional components are loosely defined. Students are informed that they will use problems to explore the dimensions of health and illness in the modern world. They are told that in very simplistic terms, issues of health and illness involve the dynamic interaction between providers and recipients of health care within institutional settings developed by individual societies in response to specific needs. Thus any health care problem can be deconstructed into such components for the purposes of exploration. This loose framework is sufficient for students to begin once the problems are distributed.

To further emphasize the student-centered nature of this course, the first meeting is a brainstorming session where students discuss what they believe to be critical issues in health care. These sessions have proved to be very lively, as the majority of the students have personal exposure to the health care system in some way. From these deliberations, a set of issues of specific interest to that class is distilled. Thus although common themes have emerged from year to year, the emphasis on different components varies annually (see Table 7.1). This gives an added flavor to the course, whose overall shape and emphasis is thus determined by the students.

The issues raised provide the annual content of the course. I write the problems based on the list, often using current issues to provide a timeliness to the course; thus there are no problem sets prepared in advance.

Table 7.1. Student-Centered Learning: Problem Areas Identified by Students During Initial Sessions of the Course

1993–94	1994–95
Health care system	Medical ethics
Native health care	Third World health
Aging	Primary health care
Rights/responsibility of the disabled	Crisis medicine
International health	Preventive medicine and public health
Support systems	Aging
Mental health	Alternative medicine
Ethics of research and practice	Appropriate technology in medicine
Financing of health care	Native health
Alternative medicine	Mental health
Training of health care professionals	Industry-academic relations
	Social structures, funding of health care

The Problems

The content of the course is to a certain extent guided by the interests of the class (examples shown in Exhibits 7.1 and 7.2). The first problem explores the relations between development, fertility, and the population crisis in the Third World. This was an expressed interest of that session of the class. To generate the discussion, I wrote the problem in the form of a commentary from a fictitious magazine (Exhibit 7.1) and distributed it during the week of the Cairo Conference. The immediacy of the issues was readily apparent as arguments presented were extensively discussed in the electronic media and the newspapers. Writing the problem in this particular format emphasizes my belief that issues can be generated from any written material.

The second example (Exhibit 7.2) is written in a more conventional scenario format. This problem was designed to stimulate the discussion of the role of technological procedures and was based on reports in newspapers discussing the variability in surgical rates across Ontario. Here again, it stemmed from an expressed desire of the students to discuss the appropriateness of technological procedures in medicine. Over the years, I have used a variety of presentation formats ranging from simulated op-eds from fictitious newspapers to data generated by experimental studies, and case reports. The problems have dealt with such diverse issues as the testing of a novel antimalarial drug in an African population, the admission of Native students to Canadian medical schools, and the differences in approaches to the drug problem in Canada and the Netherlands.

The Process in Practice

This section describes the structure of a typical session.

Brainstorming. As in the small group format, I use paper problems to raise issues, encourage participation, and generate enthusiasm. However, because of the larger class size, I take a more active role by standing at the blackboard acting as a scribe to ensure that the ideas raised are not lost.

Definition of Learning Tasks. Through considerable negotiation, the issues generated in the brainstorming session are pruned to produce clearly definable learning tasks representing the essential ideas and linkages (see examples). This phase is similar to the smaller group format, but the larger number of participants demands a greater vigilance on the part of both students and teacher to ensure that key issues are not missed. The learning tasks that emerge are not sacrosanct and the formation of the learning groups often leads to their modification. Clearly not all students participate to the same extent on all occasions. However, over the course of the year, the participation evens out.

Formation of Study Groups. The objectives of this phase are to use the learning tasks as a focus for the formation of floating groups consisting of three to five students. Each student opts to be part of a single study group for the

Exhibit 7.1. Sample Problem: An Article from a Fictitious Magazine

The following commentary was published in *Refractions*, a new magazine.

A Cradle Too Grave?
by Sonja Frei

From Cairo, September 7, 1994

On Friday, 17 June 1291, a Muslim army under the Sultan Khalil captured Acre and expelled the Franj (Christians) from Syria and all the coastal lands. The Crusades were over. Said the Arab chronicler Abu'l-Fida, "God grant that they never set foot there again!" Today, seven centuries later, a New Crusade is afoot—but this time the Pope and the Imam are fighting the ungodly together. The forces ranged against them are the voices of Western thought and reason couched in passionate terms. In the *Lancet* last year, a Zimbabwean gynecologist passionately argued against the positions taken by the Roman Catholic Church and Islam (*Lancet* 342:474, 1993).

"Leaders of Islam and the RCC (Roman Catholic Church)," he wrote, "are united in the feeling that women should not take the important decisions. On family planning there is no clear support in Koran or Bible or the clergy's position, and there are many dissenting opinions in the RCC and Islam. . . . The argument that family planning is unnatural should not be used by somebody who flies in an airplane all over the globe and has a natural tumour removed by unnatural surgery under unnatural general anaesthesia."

Their position seems ever so reasonable, but is it? Consider the comments of a Jesuit writer in the *Toronto Star* (Sept 3rd 94) "When we know the powerful spiritual meaning all peoples invest in family, children, birth etc., the Vatican asks why the UN chooses to deal with population issues in a purely scientific manner. . . . The draft does not deal seriously with the huge expenditures and profits made on weapons, interest burdens imposed by rich countries on the world's debt-laden poorest countries, wasteful overconsumption in the West or bad economic and political administration as causes—along with population increase—of poverty and underdevelopment."

I came to Cairo, ardent feminist, agnostic, rational. I heard Mrs Brundtland, Prime Minister of Norway, white middle class, eloquently arguing for women's right to abortion. I heard Benazir Bhutto, equally articulate, demanding that one cannot ignore family values and emphasising that the conference should not be seen to impose sex education and abortion on individual cultures that oppose such policies. Are we simply afraid of the sight of all those blacks and browns overrunning the earth? Maurice King talks of the "demographic trap" and notes that we romanticise children and do not even challenge the priority given to them in the allocation of desperately scarce resources (*Lancet* 341:671, 1993). Should we not place more emphasis on development rather than abortion on demand or coercive anti-birth campaigns? Can we not preserve human dignity and the human race? Or is that an impossible task?

Learning Tasks

- Relationships between development and fertility
- UN policies on population control
- Reduction of consumption as a means to tackle the population problem
- Abortion as a means to limit population

Exhibit 7.2. Sample Problem: Typical Paper Case

Unkind Cuts

Dr. Waldo Pepper, chief of surgery at St. Boniface Hospital, storms into his office waving a copy of *Thorn,* the local tabloid weekly.

Roberta Bern, an aggressive and abrasive reporter, has published an article titled "Region Surgeons Scalpel-Happy Study Finds." She had tracked down Anna S., a patient who had recently undergone laparoscopic cholecystectomy. Unfortunately, the patient had suffered bile-duct injury and other complications. Several others had suffered the same fate. Quoting a knowledgeable source within the hospital, the reporter noted that a patient was twice as likely to undergo cholecystectomy, three times as likely to have a mastectomy, and five times as likely to have a hysterectomy compared to other regions. These findings led to the inevitable conclusion that the hospital surgeons were an incompetent, money-grubbing, callous lot.

The reporter advised patients to dial their priest rather than their doctor. "The service is better, the pain is less, and you may actually live."

The president of the hospital has demanded an explanation.

The chief is livid.

"I am going to sue that ******* ***** and the ******* rag," storms the surgeon "If I find out who that ******* source is I will have his or her ***."

Note: All expletives have been deleted.

Learning Tasks

- Variability in the rates of Cesarean sections
- The profile of a surgeon
- Laparascopic surgery: technology assessment
- How to handle a scandal

---

specific problem. Considerable negotiation occurs at this stage. Quite often some tasks attract more students than others, so students must shift around until groups are approximately equal in size. Further refinement of tasks occurs at this stage, when certain tasks have no takers. A quick discussion leads to the merger of the essence of that task with another one. Each group sets up a loose contract with the rest of the class to obtain and communicate the required information. The formation of student groups changes with each group and ensures that by the end of the course the students have interacted with many different classmates. This phase is clearly different from the conventional small group format where the groups usually remain intact for extended periods of time.

Preparation for Presentations. Since the students meet in the class only once a week, they need time to prepare their presentations to be formally evaluated. In general, presentations are held two weeks after the distribution of the problem. This gives the students sufficient time to meet, discuss, find and evaluate the information, write their reports, and prepare for their presentations.

To preserve continuity, I hold a session during the intervening week to discuss any issues that require clarification or even revision. On occasion, students find that information they have acquired for their presentations could prove useful for another group and this session provides for sharing prior to the formal presentation.

Group Presentations. Presentations occur at a subsequent session. The objectives of this component are to teach students to effectively communicate the information that they have gathered and to provide a mechanism for clear expression of ideas by individual members. Here again the format diverges from the conventional small group format, where there is usually no formal presentation of information. To ensure that ample time is available for discussions, one student chairs the proceedings and ensures that the presentations keep to time.

Group Evaluations. Evaluations provide a mechanism whereby class members express their individual opinions about presentations made by each group. Each student is asked to grade the presentations and also make comments. To help them, I provide guidelines. Thus they are to give high marks for clear statements of objectives, clear and concise presentations, logical sequencing of individual sections, concepts supported by good examples, enjoyable format, precise answers to questions, and provision of new and useful information. Conversely, they are to give lower marks for rambling, discursive presentations; poor statements of objectives; poor coordination between individual sections; tedious, dull, and overlong presentations; inadequate referencing; and inability to answer questions satisfactorily.

Despite the guidelines, this component is necessarily subjective and the students are often uncomfortable. Nevertheless, I repeatedly emphasize that responsible learning involves coming to terms with subjectivity. Their marks (along with mine) are averaged to get a group mark that is allotted to each member of the group. Along with the marks, I distribute a typed sheet with the collated comments. Here again the procedure departs considerably from the small group format, where no such formal evaluation occurs.

Written Reports. Each group is required to submit a written report (one thousand words) of the presentation. The instructions are that the objectives must be clearly stated, the development of the arguments be logical, conclusions be appropriate, and referencing be adequate. I grade and comment on these reports on my own.

Student Comments

Student responses to the course have been generally favorable. Table 7.2 summarizes how three groups of students have rated the degree to which the specific aims of each element of the problem-based learning process have been met. The overall responses cluster in the upper ranges, the mode for each query being either 4 or 5. There were some elements that received mixed ratings. The largest number of scores of 3 or lower—still a relatively small proportion—were for the definition of learning tasks and the group evaluations. As noted earlier, the framing of learning tasks is not easy and involves a considerable degree of give and take. Certain issues that may appear of great interest to a particular individual may not be dealt with if the consensus deems otherwise. However, students always have the option of picking up on those elements and using them for their personal explorations.

Group evaluations are again controversial. A large number of students clearly enjoyed the opportunity to give and receive comments from others. However, some were distinctly uneasy with it. For instance, one student complained that the comments were sometimes mechanical whereas another noted that it was difficult to please everyone with one half of the class liking overheads and the other not. Another student, echoing a concern of several, noted, "People should be encouraged to put some real thought into what they write and how they mark. If people are going to evaluate they should do it responsibly." These issues were discussed several times during the course along with the importance of taking responsibility for one's comments and being as fair and constructive as possible.

Conclusions

The course that I have described set out to adapt the cardinal elements of problem-based learning to a larger group. The typical session detailed here shows close similarities to a conventional small group tutorial. The distinctions are obvious: In the brainstorming phase, the teacher plays a far more active role. The negotiations over the definition of learning tasks are far more explicit. The formation of floating groups, the formal presentations, and the group evaluations are significant departures from the conventional format. However, the essence of problem-based learning is preserved.

To retain the student-centered component of the course, I have encouraged students to be involved in setting priorities for their own learning. This,

Table 7.2. Students' Average Rating of the Degree to Which Specific Aims of Each PBL Element Were Met

	Distribution of Scores*				
	1	2	3	4	5
Brainstorming	0	0	1	18	35
Definition of learning tasks	0	0	5	26	21
Group learning	0	1	1	17	35
Group presentations	0	1	3	29	17
Group evaluations	0	1	7	17	27

*Scale: 1 = not achieved, 5 = completely achieved

however, demands that I be flexible enough to adjust to those priorities. Over the last six years, I have rarely used a problem more than once. Thus the problems are written on demand, driven by current issues, rather than prepared ahead of time.

The success of any course depends primarily on the qualities of the students and secondarily on the effort of the teachers and the support of the administration. This is particularly true of courses that promote active learning designed to create the self-centered, autonomous learner. Thus whether the procedures described will transfer well to other courses and programs is difficult to say. I began with a group of highly motivated, articulate, enthusiastic students, who reveled in the opportunity to direct their own learning. As the sole teacher for the course, I had the luxury of responding promptly to their needs with the support of the directors of the arts and sciences program. I was permitted to be as flexible as I could, provided I fulfilled my obligations. Teaching a course in this fashion requires time and effort. Apart from the contact time of three hours per week for two terms (twenty-five or twenty-six weeks), considerable time is spent researching different areas to write appropriate problems. More time is spent on marking the reports and the final essays, as well as collating the comments of the students.

The exhilaration of participating in a course with such a lively bunch of students is ample reward for all the effort. It reinforces what we often forget, that higher education is a privilege and not a right—for students and teachers alike. The price of that privilege is responsibility.

References

Albanese, M. A., and Mitchell, S. "Problem-Based Learning: A Review of Literature on Its Outcomes and Implementation Issues." *Academic Medicine,* 1993, *68* (1), 52–81.

Barrows, H. S., and Tamblyn, R. M. *Problem-Based Learning: An Approach to Medical Education.* New York: Springer, 1980.

Boud, D. *Developing Student Autonomy in Learning.* London: Kogan Page, 1988.

Boud, D., and Felleti, G. (eds.). *The Challenge of Problem-Based Learning.* New York: St. Martin's Press, 1991.

Branda, L. A. "Implementing Problem-Based Learning." *Journal of Dental Education,* 1990, *54,* 1–2.

Eisner, E. W. *The Art of Educational Evaluation: A Personal View.* London: Falmer Press, 1985.

Rangachari, P. K. "Active Learning: In Context." *American Journal of Physiology,* 1995, *268,* S75–S80.

P. K. RANGACHARI is professor in the department of medicine at McMaster University, director of the honors biology-pharmacology co-op program, and on the faculty of the arts and sciences program.

In this approach to architecture education, the design project serves as the predominant learning tool. Working individually and in small groups, students use design problems to stimulate and organize their self-directed learning of essential architectural concepts.

Time Expenditure, Workload, and Student Satisfaction in Problem-Based Learning

Arthur J. Kingsland

The central activity of an architect is design, supported by a raft of other allied professional activities. Similarly, in all architectural schools, design takes a central role, concentrating on theoretical and practical aspects of the design process. Theoretical aspects include alternate processes of design, design methods, and conceptual theories that inform designers. Students develop practical design abilities by undertaking the design stages of architectural projects. These projects are initiated with a common brief for all students, who then work together in studios and individually. With help from tutors, students determine their own direction for the project, placing emphasis on those aspects that each determines to be most important.

In 1985, the architecture faculty in the University of Newcastle (Australia) began using problem-based learning (PBL) for its courses (Maitland, 1991). This responded to a number of criticisms of the traditional architecture courses organized around separate, uncoordinated, lecture-based subjects. The new course has undergone rigorous external accreditation procedures and now receives excellent reports. It is also gaining an excellent reputation outside the university, especially from those who have contact with our graduates.

The PBL method places an emphasis on students' self-directed learning and demands that content material be integrated with all other aspects of the course. While many characteristics of PBL courses in architecture are similar to more traditional architectural courses, the Newcastle course differs in that other subject areas are fully integrated and coordinated with the design project. Students are specifically assisted in developing this ability to integrate diverse areas of knowledge. This chapter uses the architecture courses at New-castle to illustrate how PBL facilitates the integration of all aspects of architec-tural study.

PBL for Architectural Education

At the University of Newcastle, architectural design projects are central to the learning environment. Through projects, students acquire content; develop process skills; explore appropriate professional, social, and cultural attitudes; and develop a personal architectural philosophical position. Projects derived from real-world problems are tailored to suit students' learning needs. Stan-dards within the course are monitored through formal accreditation processes, internal evaluation, and the maintenance of informal and external contacts including use of part-time practitioners tutoring in the design studio where they have individual contact with students.

The architecture program uses a five-year, full-time, two-tier professional degree structure. The three-year Bachelor of Science (Architecture) is followed by a two-year Bachelor of Architecture. Each year is offered as a single inte-grated subject, that is, as Architecture 1, Architecture 2, and so on.

The central activity—architectural design—is provided by a component labeled Design Integration and supported by four learning domains—profes-sional, environmental, technical, and theoretical—providing content, process skills, and detailed application knowledge appropriate for the project type (see Figure 8.1). The component mix within these domains is monitored both by faculty and by external accreditation bodies.

The *professional domain* covers issues of professional practice including business and management skills, as well as the development of basic core sup-

Figure 8.1. Learning Domains Supporting Architectural Design

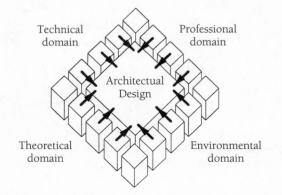

Derived from Ostwald and Chen, 1991, p. 95. Used by permission of the Australian Problem Based Learning Network.

porting skills such as architectural drawing and drafting, computer skills, communication, and presentation. Issues dealing with ecologically sustainable development and other environmental issues are addressed within the *environmental domain,* including properties of building materials and their ability to modify external climatic conditions. It also includes landscape planning and urban development. The *technical domain* provides detailed knowledge about how buildings are put together, including knowledge of laws, legal requirements, and procedures relating to buildings; structural and constructional properties of materials; understanding of how building components are joined and supported; and so on. The *theoretical domain* underpins the rest of the course, providing the philosophical basis for the practice of architecture including the study of precedents and various schools of architectural thought, the study of architectural design processes and methods, and the development a personal architectural philosophy.

Study Areas. The subject matter and learning activities within the four domains are directed toward the specific project, and delivered by methods appropriate for developing skills in self-directed and lifelong learning (Boud, 1985, 1988; Woods, 1985). Process skills, attitudinal development, and the refinement of a personal architectural philosophy are supported by generic material and assignments. The constraints and opportunities of the project are addressed by specific content, much of which is sourced by the students. Students determine for themselves the relative priority of competing demands within the project with guidance from design and study discipline tutors. Each student thus has a different mix of learning needs and time commitments.

Design Studio. Guided by their design decisions, students interpret the study area material and seek additional material where needed. Students participate in two 2.5-hour design studio sessions per week as small group tutorials (ten to fifteen students). Students discuss the work of each group member with the tutor, who provides individual help where necessary.

Initially in these sessions, students explore the scope of the project and the issues generated by the architectural brief, which contains the detailed requirements for the project. Students research the materials supplied and develop their own briefs. They analyze the client's information and investigate the site, recording existing conditions and influences on the site such as vegetation, amenities, views, noise sources, climatic influences, and anything else relevant to the development. Students also meet the client to determine less tangible aspects of the development, such as the image that the client wants to convey or the priority to be given to different aspects of the project. Tutors help students identify individual learning needs dictated by their briefs. In addition, students determine a suitable conceptual basis for their project and are guided in articulating this concept and developing it into a workable architectural design.

Integration. Strong emphasis is placed on integrating supporting content material with the design project. Students work through each project using a holistic approach, but hierarchically subdivide the project's components into manageable chunks. Architectural projects are very complex, requiring consideration of both abstract qualities and complex interactions across a number of disciplines. Competing demands (such as safety, comfort, environmental impact, and so on) are prioritized with influences as diverse as historical precinct requirements, structural and mechanical systems requirements, environmental demands, user requirements, and local council development orders, to name only a few. Consideration is given to the influence of one demand on the rest of the project. Students study individual components within each study discipline, then integrate this material into their scheme to support their design proposals. The study disciplines are the individual domains of content coordinated and delivered by experts in each field of knowledge.

Study Discipline Content Requirements. The course must meet standards set by external accreditation bodies representing the profession, academia, and the Architects' Registration Board. Mandatory content requirements are incorporated into the projects by careful design of the architectural briefs that initiate each project. Architectural projects are very large and complex, and students therefore need clear objectives, definition of project scope, and guidance about where emphasis should be placed. Even with this careful structuring, only two to five projects are tackled per year, although a number of short projects (up to one week in duration) allow the investigation of more theoretical aspects of architectural design.

PBL and Traditional Architectural Education: Similarities and Differences

In many respects, PBL and traditional architectural programs appear similar in that theoretical and practical aspects of the design process are investigated, as are supporting disciplines that inform a designer. Most schools of architecture claim that the design project offers the vehicle for discovering the design process and other subjects provide the supporting information to help the design process.

Traditional Architectural Education. Integration of supporting material with the design project in traditional architectural programs is left entirely to the student and little attention is devoted to this integration ability when assessing design proposals. In design studios, each student demands individual design advice. Most students receive only a few minutes of attention each week from their tutors. Final proposal presentations require detailed resolution of the design. In design tutorials, there is never enough time to resolve these details as well as discuss larger issues of architectural theory and its application to the design. Tutorials thus generally concentrate on the larger questions of the profession, on architectural theory, societal expectations, and on each student's philosophical position related to the current project.

PBL Architectural Education. At Newcastle, the central design activity is accommodated by the provision of Design Integration projects. The word *integration* in the label is deliberate. The integration of information from various study disciplines is considered a necessary condition for a true understanding of the parameters of the design process. In traditional architectural programs, content material covered in study disciplines is *not* integrated into design projects, is *not* coordinated with design projects, and usually is *not* addressed as part of the design assessment; PBL stresses all three.

For each design project to support the integration of information from a number of disciplines as part of the design process, a careful timetabling effort is required. Each project is designed by a coordinator called the year manager, assisted by the teaching team having contact with that year. Learning goals are identified appropriate to the developmental sequence of the whole course. Study discipline coordinators identify which projects are appropriate for the study of issues within the domain of their discipline. The year manager coordinates these requirements, identifies areas of common interest, negotiates contact session allocations and students' workload commitments with each consultant, then refines the detailed documentation for the project.

In summary, the PBL implementation in architecture at Newcastle is similar to other architectural schools in that the central activity is the design project, and students determine their own priorities, direction, and emphasis. The difference is that in PBL integration of study discipline content is considered a specific part of the design process and is directly addressed in design tutorials.

Outcomes. Outcomes of using the PBL method integrating study discipline material in context include the following:

- Design solutions are more realistic and buildable.
- All material covered at a given time contributes to a common direction, rather than having disjointed and competing educational demands.
- Learning of study discipline material is easier because the relevance of the material is much clearer.
- Students are better prepared for practice and better able to begin productive work because they understand the need for, and are capable of, integrating diverse areas of knowledge on complex projects. Employers confirm this observation.

A specific issue addressed by the faculty was development of students' abilities in personal and written communication. A high level of communication is now demanded using the processes of interviewing clients, users, and others involved in the project design and implementation stages; intragroup interaction during design tutorials; documentation of proposed designs using drawings, reports, models and other media; and verbal presentation of design proposals and conceptual ideas to a design jury. Group tutorials are used and, when appropriate, team research and development processes as well. This group work helps students develop an understanding of group dynamics and appropriate team skills.

Project Selection. Project selection is determined mostly by the scale and complexity of the project. Students begin with simple buildings having only a few spaces and simple relationships between the spaces. Projects increase in size and architectural complexity, but also in the number and complexity of side issues. In later years, political, societal, and ethical issues are addressed as part of the design process.

Determining the scope of a specific project is a more difficult aspect of project selection. Only a fraction of any project can ever be addressed by the students. For example, the proposals are not actually turned into real buildings, so students do not experience the full effect of decisions made during the design stages or the complexity of personnel and project management processes. In project design, consideration is given to progress in the students' development, time constraints imposed by the educational system, and the demands on the profession by society. Factors considered in this selection are the sequential development with each study discipline, the need to address specific issues, and the application of understanding developed in previous projects.

Faculty review and agree on the overall themes for each level of the course during course planning meetings. Year managers propose broad descriptions of and timetables for projects and negotiate with staff providing supporting study disciplines for specific aspects to be included within each project. The year manager creates a sequence of projects to address professional issues and to help students develop design and research abilities. Staff members coordinating study disciplines determine appropriate places within the complete degree program to address each knowledge area and issue. The year manager and study area staff then develop materials for presentation to students during the progress of the project. The project materials (called the *brief*) are designed to provide leads and guidance about where emphasis should be placed in addressing the needs of the particular project.

Time Commitments

Problem-based learning methods have often been criticized because of the way they increase staff and student workloads. Lovie-Kitchin (1991) reports that optometry students felt that "problem based learning required more time, but fewer feel that it is too time consuming" (p. 199). Time constraints cause complications for sharing or discussing information. Lovie-Kitchin (1991) comments that considerable work is required to prepare comprehensive resource information and provide timely feedback. Time is also needed to design the new approach.

Cawley (1991) surveyed mechanical engineering students and observed underreporting of time expenditure, noting "students could frequently be heard discussing the problems in the coffee room, an almost unheard of occurrence on conventional courses, and this valuable peer learning may not have appeared on their estimates" (p. 183). Cawley's observations were mirrored in our time expenditure investigations with architecture students at Newcastle.

Research indicates that PBL need not demand time increases (Kingsland,

1993; Cowdroy and Kingsland, 1992, 1994). Ideally, there should be no increase in student or staff load, but this requires constant vigilance to foresee significant workload components and the flexibility to accommodate changes that arise during the progress of each project.

Staff members have been aware from the first stages of implementation of the PBL course in 1985 that as integration is an extra component added to every project, they must reduce the content to ensure that students are not overloaded. This is constantly monitored, but is still of major concern to the students.

Student Evaluation

Students identify their time commitments as part of the project documentation process and are actively encouraged to report problems they foresee, allowing adjustments to be made as each project progresses. Ad hoc comments during design tutorial sessions are communicated back to the year manager for action.

Architecture 1 students maintain Reflective Design Journals to aid in the development of design and critical analysis skills. Comments in these journals highlight times of high stress due either to the accumulation of assignments or to time management problems (resulting from personal circumstances or institutional demands). The journals are a valuable evaluation instrument.

End-of-project student evaluation questionnaires are used to gauge students' opinion about aspects of the PBL implementation. Part of this questionnaire addresses timing of activities and time requirements to complete projects.

At the end of each semester, two additional formal feedback sessions occur. Individual end-of-semester interviews with each student are conducted to review progress, and a separate review with an independent facilitator is also conducted with representatives from all years. Comments are sought to identify where the course has helped and hindered progress. This feedback is used by the year manager to rectify shortcomings when planning activities for the next semester or year.

Time Expenditure and Workload

Recent surveys of Australian tertiary graduates (Graduate Careers Council of Australia, 1993, 1994) examined students' opinion of course experiences using a set of twenty-five items grouped into six categories:

- Good teaching
- Clear goals and standards
- Appropriate assessment
- Appropriate workload
- Generic skills
- Overall satisfaction

In the 1994 Course Experience Survey of 1993 graduates, the Newcastle graduates rated the PBL course at the top of all fourteen Australian Architecture courses for Clear Goals and Standards and Overall Satisfaction, tied at the top for Generic Skills, third of fourteen for Good Teaching and Appropriate Assessment. On the negative side, however, they clearly indicated dissatisfaction with Appropriate Workload, placing it twelfth out of fourteen. Similar results were reported from the 1993 survey.

Student and staff workloads have been of concern from the time of the original conversion of the architectural course from traditional methods to PBL. This concern, allied with the clear message from the Course Experience Survey, prompted us to investigate workloads in more depth. A survey was designed with advice from staff and students, then given to all students in all years of the course. The questionnaire consisted of a number of true-false and Likert scale items, open-ended questions, and space for additional comments for each of a number of components of the workload issue (Kingsland, 1994).

Approximately 70 percent of the enrolled students responded to the survey. They indicated that time expended is determined primarily by the need to undertake assignments and other set work, there was little time to pursue individual learning needs outside of those dictated by submission requirements (the respondents in three of the four years surveyed were almost unanimous on this item), and time expenditure was influenced strongly by the motivation to do well. The average of the students' (n = 131) self-rating of their motivation was 2.37 on a 0 to 3 scale (poor to very high), indicating a fairly high level of motivation. Generally, students did not think that the tasks were too difficult, but that the time available to complete the tasks was insufficient. Although many suggested that developing better time management skills would help, they saw project planning and coordination as the major problem, rather than their self-management ability.

Conclusion

One major finding of the workload survey is that despite high workloads, students are very satisfied with the PBL teaching method. The other major outcome is that the total workload, although high, is not the problem. Of more concern to students are the timing of activities, the availability of complete workload information at the beginning of projects, and the availability of appropriate, dedicated working spaces.

The survey findings coincided with an evaluation of staff time commitments resulting in recognition of the need for changes to reduce the pressure on staff and students. Staff need time for research, administration, and other academic contributions and the students need free time for reflection and consolidation of learning.

The student and staff workload review was coordinated with a major review of relative weightings of study disciplines in response to changing professional and societal demands. This helped us identify existing problem areas and remove extraneous work requirements.

Time expenditure is only one component of workload and this must be recognized when designing or reviewing a PBL curriculum. Care should be exercised that all components are coordinated with the central project scenario and contribute to the students' learning needs. It does seem, however, that the PBL process holds great promise for the integration of architectural studies with professional needs and values.

References

Boud, D. "Problem-Based Learning in Perspective." In D. Boud (ed.), *Problem-Based Learning in Education for the Professions*. Sydney: Higher Education Research and Development Society of Australasia, 1985.

Boud, D. *Developing Student Autonomy in Learning*. London: Kogan Page, 1988.

Cawley, P. "A Problem-Based Module in Mechanical Engineering." In D. Boud and G. Feletti (eds.), *The Challenge of Problem-Based Learning*. New York: St. Martin's Press, 1991.

Cowdroy, R. M., and Kingsland, A. J. "Problem-Based Learning Is Not Resource Extravagant." In M. S. Parer (ed.), *Research and Development in Higher Education*. Vol. 15. Sydney: Higher Education Research and Development Society of Australasia, 1992.

Cowdroy, R. M., and Kingsland, A. J. "Decompressing the Timetables in Problem-Based Learning." In G. Ryan, P. J. Little, and I. Dunn (eds.), *Research and Development in Higher Education*. Vol.16. Sydney: Higher Education Research and Development Society of Australasia, 1994.

Graduate Careers Council of Australia. *1993 Course Experience Survey: Preliminary Results for Individual Universities by Minor Field of Study*. Sydney: Graduate Careers Council of Australia, 1993.

Graduate Careers Council of Australia. *1994 Course Experience Survey: Preliminary Results for Individual Universities by Minor Field of Study*. Sydney: Graduate Careers Council of Australia, 1994.

Kingsland, A. J. "Problem-Based Learning: Efficient, Affordable and Stress-Free Implementation." In G. Ryan (ed.), *Research and Development in Problem Based Learning*. Vol. 1. Sydney: Australian Problem Based Learning Network, 1993.

Kingsland, A. J. *Workload Study—Architecture Course*. (Internal Document.) Newcastle, Australia: Department of Architecture, University of Newcastle, 1994.

Lovie-Kitchin, J. "Problem-Based Learning in Optometry." In D. Boud and G. Feletti (eds.), *The Challenge of Problem-Based Learning*. New York: St. Martin's Press, 1991.

Maitland, B. S. "Problem Based Learning for an Architecture Degree." In D. Boud and G. Feletti (eds.), *The Challenge of Problem-Based Learning*. New York: St. Martin's Press, 1991.

Ostwald, M. J., and Chen, S. E. "Marginalisation of Theoretical Issues in a Professional PBL Course: A Structural or Attitudinal Problem." In S. E. Chen, R. M. Cowdroy, A. J. Kingsland, and M. J. Ostwald (eds.), *Reflections on Problem Based Learning*. Sydney: Australian Problem Based Learning Network, 1991.

Woods, D. "Problem-Based Learning and Problem Solving." In D. Boud (ed.), *Problem-Based Learning in Education for the Professions*. Sydney: Higher Education Research and Development Society of Australasia, 1985.

ARTHUR J. KINGSLAND is assistant dean and a senior lecturer in the department of architecture at the University of Newcastle, Australia.

We describe an approach to teaching calculus that emphasizes
problem solving through its stress on in-class activities and
context-rich projects.

An Active Approach to Calculus

Stan Seltzer, Steve Hilbert, John Maceli, Eric Robinson,
Diane Schwartz

Picture this: On the first day of Calculus One, the instructor tells the students that as she tosses a piece of chalk into the air, each student is to draw a graph of the height of the chalk from the floor in terms of time with the height of the chalk along the vertical axis. The instructor then tosses a piece of chalk into the air, catches it, and gives the students about a minute to draw their graphs. Then the students exchange their graphs and are asked to write a brief paragraph describing the position of the chalk based on the graph they are looking at (not their own recollection); each paragraph should include the maximum height of the chalk and the length of time the chalk was in the air if this can be determined from the graph. The students receive their own graphs back and the class has a short discussion about communicating information, and in particular about the importance of scales and units for graphs. Finally the instructor tosses the chalk again and each student draws a graph. The instructor may expand on this activity by tossing the chalk to bounce off the ceiling, dropping the chalk, or other variations.

In fact, this is the way we begin our calculus course. We want our students to see in their very first class that their active involvement in solving problems, small and large, will be a central feature of the course.

Our Calculus One/Two courses form a mainstream two-semester calculus sequence that mathematics majors take. However, most of the students are in the sciences, health professions, business, music, communications, and liberal arts. Classes meet four times per week for fourteen weeks in sections of about twenty-five students. The topics taught during the year are the central calculus topics: limits and continuity, differentiation, integration, series, differential equations.

We began to reconsider calculus in 1988 when the "calculus reform movement" was gathering momentum (Douglas, 1986; Steen, 1988). Along with many colleagues, we were not satisfied with our course. Most students were learning techniques, but relatively few were able to apply these in subsequent work. The emergence of symbolic computing systems (such as Maple, Mathematica, and Derive) and graphing calculators had raised serious questions about how much emphasis ought to be placed on hand calculation. In addition, we hoped to increase the number of students who would continue in mathematics.

After consulting with colleagues in other disciplines, we established goals for the course: focus clearly on the central concepts of calculus and provide for effective student learning, focus on higher-order thinking skills, emphasize the unity of calculus, and improve attitudes toward mathematics. Our concern about problem solving led us to incorporate projects into our course, and to build a foundation for these we developed our active approach.

What makes our course active? We frequently have our students work on activities in the classroom, sometimes individually and sometimes in groups. In addition, we use large problems or projects, often open-ended, to motivate or introduce topics, to integrate or reinforce concepts, and to enrich the syllabus. Students work on projects outside of class in groups of three, spending two to three weeks on each project.

We use a spiral approach in teaching our course, returning frequently to a number of recurring threads, such as graphs, distance and velocity, multiple representations of functions, estimation and approximation, and modeling. Most problems we pose include multiple concepts, forcing students to connect topics. These threads are a source of continual review by which we emphasize the unity of calculus.

On the other hand, many aspects of this course are quite typical. When students are not doing activities (about half the time), we lecture (fairly interactively) and answer questions from students. We assign homework daily, give quizzes regularly (every week or two), and give one or two exams as well as a comprehensive final. We encourage our students to use graphing calculators.

Activities for Calculus One

Let us return to the Chalk Toss and discuss what it accomplishes. First, the students learn that their involvement as more than notetakers is expected. In particular, exchanging graphs convinces the class that each student is expected to draw a graph and write a commentary. We also encourage their participation by walking around the classroom as they are working, asking leading questions to students who are hesitant or are having difficulty. Second, the students model a real-life situation by drawing a graph. They have also translated a mathematical concept (a graph) into a verbal concept (a paragraph), experiencing in a concrete way that a function has more than one representation. We stress heavily that in addition to representing a function symbolically as a formula, we may represent a function graphically and numerically as well as verbally and physically. Finally, the students have reviewed coordinates, scales, and units in a meaningful context.

As much as possible, we use activities to change the classroom climate from one where the students sit and listen to one where the students are active; but note that we are also introducing and clarifying material at the same time. In this case, student problem solving has almost completely replaced the lecture; the mathematical topics addressed all arise in the context of the activity. The instructor can readily identify difficulties or misconceptions that the students may have and focus discussion on them. Having observed the students at work, the instructor finds it relatively easy to have the class contribute much of the explanation. To follow up, we typically assign the students to sketch the graph of a different but related problem, such as of a flag being raised and lowered.

The Classroom Walk is another activity that builds on the Chalk Toss. This activity is usually part of the second class of Calculus One. Each student is asked to draw a graph of the position of the instructor relative to an origin (a mark on the board) as the instructor walks in front of the class during a specified time interval. The walk could be reconstructed using either the distance or velocity graph. This introduces one of the core ideas of the calculus, finding derivatives and integrals, in a graphical context. The idea of identifying distance-velocity pairs is revisited in greater depth throughout the course. Finally, the students understand that position is maximized when the velocity changes from positive to negative, one specific instance of the first-derivative test.

Once again the activity involves students' modeling an everyday situation using a graph. The concept of slope is reviewed in a meaningful context. A variation of this activity also lets the students see a correspondence from a mathematical object to the real world: from a position graph, one can describe, or actually perform, the corresponding walk. In this way, the students are learning what mathematicians call modeling, the process of taking a real problem, translating it to a mathematical situation, analyzing the mathematics, and finally interpreting the solution in the original context. If the explanation provided by the model does not fit, the process is repeated.

Here is another example of an activity:

At time $t = 0$, water begins to flow from a hose into an empty tank at the rate of 40 liters per minute. This flow rate is held constant for two minutes, at which time the tank contains 80 liters. At that time ($t = 2$), the water pressure is gradually reduced, until at time $t = 4$ the flow rate is 5 liters per minute. This flow rate is held constant for the final two-minute period, at which time ($t = 6$) the tank contains 120 liters. Suppose also that a pump is started at time $t = 2$ and water is pumped out at a rate of 15 liters per minute. Draw a graph of the volume of water that has been pumped into the tank and, on the same graph, of the volume of water that has been pumped out. Show how to find on your graph the point at which the water level in the tank is at a maximum.

This introduction to maximizing a function is presented around the third week of Calculus One. In this case, first students must graph the volume of water entering the tank; then they graph the volume leaving the tank. Their problem is to determine when the difference is greatest.

A number of important ideas appear in this activity. For example, in one part of the activity students are asked to draw a line whose slope is the average flow rate during the six-minute period. Thus they must recall that the average over an interval is the slope of a line. They are also asked questions about the instantaneous flow rate, which is the slope of the tangent to the curve (the derivative at a point). They need to know what the graph of volume will be when the flow rate is constant and when the flow rate is decreasing. Students continually need to interpret verbal descriptions and graph the phenomenon described, again confronting the thread of multiple representation of functions.

This example illustrates the spiral approach in several ways. Students confront some concepts already encountered, such as average rate and instantaneous rate. Through this new application, they gain a deeper appreciation for the generality of these concepts and the power of abstraction. Similarly, the concept of concavity and its relationship to rates is reinforced. Ideas that are now familiar are revisited. On the other hand, the notion of optimization, introduced briefly in the Classroom Walk, is significantly broadened to a difference. (Here the quantity being optimized is a difference.) Later in the course, once the derivative has been defined and students have results about the derivative of a difference, the Water Tank provides an example of an application. This pedagogical strategy of working from the concrete to the abstract represents a vast departure from the traditional definition-theorem-proof-application style of presentation. Students seem to generalize better when they work from specific to general and then back to a new specific than when they start with a theorem.

Beyond introducing an important mathematical principle, this activity supports our goal of improving problem-solving skills. This problem does not have a unique correct answer because students can interpret "gradually reduced" in different ways and obtain different curves. They become aware of how modeling assumptions can affect their solution.

The goal of stressing unity is supported in a number of ways. First, relationships between rates and aggregates are needed to produce appropriate graphs. Second, students are reminded of various interpretations of rates (average and instantaneous). In addition, this provides another example of the importance of being able to analyze a verbal description and translate it into a graph (multiple representation of functions).

To summarize, our students develop a deeper awareness and ownership of important concepts in the course by working on activities, a basic tenet of the constructive approach to learning. One aspect of the spiral approach is that we often compare activities and projects to one another—many of them illustrate the same general principles. For example, when treating basic applications to economics, students are reminded of the water tank. At this point they know that marginals are rates, so the concept that profit is maximized when marginal revenue ("flow rate in") equals marginal cost ("flow rate out") is familiar. Also, through the activities, we teach modeling and how to use a top-down approach to solve problems. The class activities are designed to accustom the students to active participation in the course and to introduce and reinforce important material and methods.

Projects

Activities constitute in-class problem solving; out-of-class problems take the form of projects. Over the course of a semester, we assign three or four projects to be completed by teams of three students over a period of two to three weeks. Some of these projects are included in Hilbert and others (1994) and one is discussed in Hilbert and others (1993).

For example, the project Tidal Flows emphasizes graphical calculus, estimation, and modeling. The project is staged so that each student group takes the role of a team of consulting engineers studying the flow of water from a river into a large lake. Data are presented in the form of a graph detailing the amount of water that has flowed into the lake from the river as a function of time for a fourteen-day period. The team must submit a report to their client that addresses several questions, the answers to which are to be obtained from the graphical representation of the data. The questions require individual as well as team problem-solving, and put many of the in-class activities into a real-world context.

In addition to other questions, we ask the team to respond to open-ended questions posed by the client, who is considering the construction of a small hydroelectric plant on the lake. Minimum and maximum flow rates that would allow the plant to operate and a minimum flow rate at which the plant could operate at full capacity are given. The team is asked to provide two examples of flow curves that would be good for the plant. The consultants must explain in writing what is meant by the term good and what their graphs mean in terms of the river and the lake. Lastly, the team is given constraints for peak load periods each day and asked to draw two graphs that would be beneficial for plant operations. The team must explain any differences between these two graphs and the two graphs they provided in response to the previous question. This part of the project, in particular, forces students to reconcile graphical representation of functions with verbal or written representation of functions. Placing the students as consultants and the realistic nature of the project help improve student attitudes toward mathematics.

Implementation

Each project centers on at least one important concept or result. Focusing our students' attention for an extended period of time on those ideas helps them learn more effectively. The projects are presented in such a way as to require some analysis. They are not strictly computational; they do require computational skills, but they enable the students to see calculations as the nuts and bolts of a larger problem-solving process.

We believe that it is best to assign the first project early in the course. This emphasizes that projects are an integral part of the course and helps students develop significant problem-solving skills that they can bring to bear on other elements of the course. The first projects are designed to move the students through a large problem. We are insistent about meeting with the student groups as they work on their first project. As students progress through the course, they tend to take the responsibility to consult with management, that is, check with us about questions they might have. They become more independent as they gain experience.

For projects, we assign students to groups based on very practical matters, such as where people live or on similarity of schedules. We change the groups at least once during the semester to give the students the opportunity to get to know several others in the class well and to give us the chance to fix problem groups. Sometimes project groups work in class where we can observe and make suggestions about group dynamics.

In our courses, the team receives a single grade on the group parts of the project. In some cases, there are individual parts that receive a grade separate from the team grade. Most of the grade is based on how well the teams answer the questions posed. We also reward creative ideas. Because there are significant written reports involved, the manner of presentation is taken into account as well.

Large projects develop and unify the most important concepts of calculus. The projects we assign are much longer than most textbook problems. The solutions often involve several different concepts. Finally, students gain an appreciation for the value of mathematics—its universality and power—while also beginning to see mathematics as a creative discipline based on their work on the projects. Realistic projects and activities convince the students that calculus has relevance beyond the classroom. Working on projects builds students' confidence in their ability to solve problems. In preparing their project reports—often staged in the role of a consultant—they learn the importance of communicating in mathematics.

Summary and Conclusions

While our course and most other so-called reform calculus courses place somewhat less emphasis on computational skills than traditional courses, the importance of students' understanding central concepts (differentiation, integration, approximation) has increased. Indeed, one major difference between reform courses and traditional courses is that in the newer courses the concepts, rather than the techniques, are central. Of course, we do expect our students to learn standard techniques that have always been part of a calculus course, such as finding derivatives, finding relative maxima and minima, determining the equation of a line tangent to a curve, finding antiderivatives, computing definite integrals, and solving differential equations. However, in contrast to more traditional courses, our students see that calculations are only one aspect of problem solving.

Among other things, problem solving involves problem analysis, developing an approach to a problem, synthesizing relevant ideas, and clearly articulating a solution. These are precisely the skills needed to develop solutions to our projects. The projects focus the students' attention on a problem that does not have a five-minute solution or even a five-hour solution; thus students also learn persistence, another important aspect of problem solving. Projects are often open-ended, which encourages relativistic thinking.

Our approach, with its stress on student problem-solving, gives students practice with techniques. Their motivation for developing symbol skills is to obtain answers to problems that have some meaning to them. The use of multiple representation of functions provides enough concrete examples so students can understand the theory.

Among the most important problem-solving strategies we teach is the top-down approach. Analogous to outlining a paper before beginning the actual writing, a top-down approach to a large-scale problem consists of identifying smaller subproblems that need to be solved. If these subproblems are not manageable, they are broken down into smaller components, and so on. We emphasize the need to put solutions back together because we have observed a tendency for students to become mired in details and lose sight of their main problem.

Other key features of our course are also important in preparing students to successfully complete projects. Activities provide students with ample opportunities to practice solving smaller problems. Multiple representation of functions gives students alternative ways of approaching problems. Graphs are easiest to start with and are particularly helpful for qualitative and global behavior.

We believe that working in groups on projects also builds problem-solving skills. Collaborating with their classmates engages the students' natural curiosity and increases their interest. Working together encourages them to work harder and better. In fact, cooperative work with good, motivated students bolsters the performance of weaker students. Meanwhile, explaining things to their peers gives strong students a deeper understanding. The support students receive from their teammates, as well as the peer pressure they may experience, enables them to accomplish things that they could not achieve alone. Finally, there is a much greater willingness for students in groups to consider and try different approaches to a problem. This helps overcome the "I don't know where to start" syndrome to which some students are prone.

We have observed that the students become more independent as a result of the experience they gain in thinking about problems. The projects engage the curiosity of the good students and challenge them, but this does not come at the expense of average and weaker students. Our approach is quite different from any mathematics that students have taken previously. It diminishes the disadvantage that students may have if they have not seen some calculus and it maintains the interest of students who have. The approach also changes the students' attitudes toward mathematics. Our experience has shown that some students become more interested and involved in mathematics because of this approach.

In our course, students learn that mathematics is a process, not just the performing of calculations. Our active approach emphasizes that mathematical thinking is a useful method of comprehending the world.

References

Douglas, R. (ed.). *Toward a Lean and Lively Calculus—Report of the Conference/Workshop to Develop Curriculum and Teaching Methods for Calculus at the College Level.* Washington, D.C.: MAA Notes 6, 1986.

Hilbert, S., Maceli, J., Robinson, E., Schwartz, D., and Seltzer, S. "Calculus: An Active Approach with Projects." *PRIMUS,* 1993, 3 (1), 71–82.

Hilbert, S., Maceli, J., Robinson, E., Schwartz, D., and Seltzer, S. *Calculus—An Active Approach with Projects.* New York: Wiley, 1994.

Steen, L. (ed.). *Calculus for a New Century—A Pump, Not a Filter.* Washington, D.C.: MAA Notes 8, 1988.

STAN SELTZER, STEVE HILBERT, JOHN MACELI, ERIC ROBINSON, *and* DIANE SCHWARTZ *are faculty members in the department of mathematics and computer science at Ithaca College in Ithaca, New York.*

*Our new program in chemical engineering improved students'
marks as well as their response to the learning environment,
problem-solving skills, and lifetime learning skills. Alumni
and employer response has been very positive.*

Problem-Based Learning for Large Classes in Chemical Engineering

Donald R. Woods

Three educational problems have motivated our move toward problem-based learning (PBL) in the chemical engineering program at McMaster University. First, we continually feel pressured to add more and more specialty courses into an already crammed curriculum. Environment, waste reduction, microelectronics, biotechnology, biomedical engineering—these are but a few of the options we should include. Second, since the late 1970s, we have struggled to address a perceived mismatch between the needs of the chemical engineering industry and the level of our graduates in such process skills as problem solving, interpersonal communication, group and team participation, coping with change, and self-assessment. Reports emphasized that our graduates lacked these process skills despite our best intentions to develop them (Rush, Krmpotic, and Evers, 1985; Bradford School of Technical Management, 1984; Sparkes, 1989; Resnick, 1987). Third, pressure for educational accountability for the learning achieved by our students shifted the focus from teaching to learning. Research pointed to the advantages of using active and cooperative learning environments, of providing prompt feedback, and of developing environments that nurture success and take into account individual learning preferences (Chickering and Gamson, 1987). Other research suggested the advantages of using problem-based versus subject-based learning in terms of the types of cognitive structures developed by the students (Norman and Schmidt, 1992).

Note: I am pleased to acknowledge the input from the students I have worked with over the past ten years with PBL and from Andy Hrymak, Fred Hall, Carolyn Eyles, Wendy Duncan-Hewitt, Chris Knapper, Tracy Pringle-Clarke, and Heather Wright.

In the early 1980s, contrary to the trend of adding more courses, our department of chemical engineering at McMaster University decided to offer fewer courses and to focus explicitly on developing students' lifetime learning skills so that our graduates could, in the future, effectively and efficiently acquire new knowledge as needed. Small group, self-directed problem-based learning seemed an attractive curricular option for promoting lifetime learning skills, providing an opportunity to develop process skills and improve student learning. The more we explored this option, the more excited we became. This chapter describes our use of PBL, nine issues of concern, and how we addressed them.

Use of Problem-Based Learning

We use PBL as part of two courses in chemical engineering: one problem in a junior-level course and five problems in a senior-level course (Woods, 1991). Each course has about thirty to fifty students with one instructor. Hence, we use five to ten tutorless groups with five students per group (Woods and others, 1995).

Each problem is studied for one week. The students are required to submit journal reports on their progress in the PBL tutorless groups. For each problem, the students hold three formal meetings: a goals meeting, a teaching meeting, and an elaboration and feedback meeting. Student-generated learning issues are validated by the instructor during the goals meeting. Before encountering the first PBL unit, the students receive about fifty hours of workshop-style training in group process skills.

Nine Issues of Concern

The major issues we encountered were acceptance by faculty and by students, how and when to develop problem-solving skills, how to work effectively with tutorless groups, how to help students cope with competing demands from concurrent conventional courses, and how to maintain a positive learning environment. We also planned to proactively address three possible weaknesses of PBL suggested in the medical education literature (Albanese and Mitchell, 1993).

Gaining Departmental Faculty Acceptance. When we started discussing curriculum revision, we all saw the need to add new courses to develop the process skills valued by our alumni and their employers, to integrate the required design project more effectively into the program, to improve the sequence of laboratories, to eliminate unnecessary overlap among courses, and to take more of a systems approach. In a department of fifteen faculty members, about half enthusiastically endorsed the addition of four required courses to develop process skills, one of which would use PBL. Other faculty members were willing to allow this to proceed. If our curriculum revision had focused only on implementing PBL, I doubt if we would have been successful.

PBL was one of six major adjustments in the overall curriculum. Furthermore, initially, it was a small component of one senior-level course.

After seven years of experience with the PBL format, the positive student response led to the spread of PBL to one junior-level course. I expect that this trend will continue, with PBL being used in more and more courses. The move to PBL was also influenced by the positive student response to a new theme school at McMaster that uses this approach starting in the sophomore year (described in Chapter Seven). A further factor in gaining faculty acceptance was our willingness to consider a fifteen-year time frame before we would expect to see measurable effects.

Hence, we addressed the lack of faculty commitment to PBL by including PBL as a small part of an overall curriculum change, by being satisfied with a few faculty willing to support the idea with the remaining faculty willing to let it happen, by using the positive student response as a force to increase the PBL content as the program evolved, and by taking a long-term view.

Gaining Student Acceptance. Students are concerned that any new approach will cause their grades to drop. We help our students adjust to new expectations by taking curricular time to describe the conditions that promote learning, to show how PBL embodies most of these, and to tell success stories from alumni about this approach. We run workshops on managing change, using Perry's inventory (1970) to help individuals identify the amount of change in attitude this new approach will take, and to help them adjust to the new learning environment (Woods, 1994, 1995a, 1995b). In addition, we use class ombudspersons to help monitor the students' reaction to the new learning environment. This takes class time. But the time is well spent; here is an example of what happens if such time is not taken. A colleague shifted a part of his course to PBL. He did not rationalize this change to the students. He did not explain the shift in his role from traditional teacher-talker-lecturer to facilitator-coach-tutor. Based on the negative student evaluations and student response to his efforts, he now claims he will never use PBL again. But PBL is not at fault; the way he introduced it is at fault.

How and When to Develop the Processing Skills Required. For students to be effective with a small group PBL approach, they should already have reasonable problem-solving, interpersonal and group behavior, self-assessment, and learning skills. Research has shown that these processing skills are not developed by merely giving the students an opportunity to apply the skills (Norman and Schmidt, 1992; Woods, 1993). Therefore, we develop the students' processing skills through explicit training programs before the PBL program begins (Woods, Crowe, Taylor, and Wood, 1984). Such skill development serves two purposes: students develop skills valued by employers and also gain the tools to work effectively in tutorless groups for the PBL components of the program.

Working with Tutorless Student Groups and Monitoring Their Accountability. Adapting the PBL approach to a large classes of thirty to fifty students with one faculty member poses two constraints: how to help the

groups deal effectively with difficulties, and how to make the students accountable for their actions. The difficulties we encountered in tutorless groups usually do not occur in tutored groups. These include such issues as attendance,
student concerns that not everyone is doing a fair share, and accountability.
Our approach is to make all contributions visible. Each student writes a journal documenting participation in PBL activities. Although such documentation can require a lot of time by both the students and the teacher, I am able
to minimize the time by using standard formats for both the student write-up
and the marking, limiting the amount of written reflection that can be sub-
mitted, using in-class time to complete the reflection, and using group reflections.

**Using PBL in the Context of a Predominantly Conventional Curricu-
lum.** If only part of a course or only one course is PBL, then students tend to
meet the demands of tests and assignments in other courses before working
on PBL responsibilities. To offset this tendency, we use many small problems
with a continual and rapid turn-around of each problem. For example, the
problem is presented on Monday. The students identify issues, prioritize, create learning objectives and distribute the learning tasks during a one- to two-
hour session. They are to learn the information and then teach each other on
Wednesday or Thursday in the teaching meeting. Friday, they give feedback to
each other by posing and working example problems based on the new knowledge that they have gained. Thus, the full cycle is completed in one week.
When a problem is stretched out over longer periods, I have found that the
students tend to procrastinate and do all of the learning in the several days
before the teaching meeting.

Monitoring for a Positive Learning Environment. We use ombuds-
people, change management workshops, Perry's inventory, and continual faculty monitoring to ensure that a positive learning environment occurs in our
program. The students' assessment, as measured by the Course Perceptions
Questionnaire (Knapper, 1994; Ramsden, 1983), is significantly more positive
for PBL (mean of 29.68) than for a control group of engineering students in a
conventional program (mean of 16.2).

Adjusting the Knowledge and Skills to be Learned. Vernon and Blake
(1993) and Albanese and Mitchell (1993) conclude that on tests of factual
recall and factual information, PBL students perform less well than students in
traditional programs. In PBL, we ask students to learn subject knowledge and
to acquire lifetime learning skills, problem-solving strategies, group skills, self-
assessment skills, and communication skills. Testing them only on subject
knowledge is inappropriate. We need to assess what we believe are the entire
range of knowledge and the skills being developed.

Albanese and Mitchell (1993) suggest that about 20 percent less subject
knowledge can be covered in a PBL course than in a conventional, lecture-
based course. To address this potential problem, we converted the processing
skills to valued outcomes. We assess them and make their acquisition part of
the grade for the program. We attempted to reduce the core fundamentals in

chemical engineering so that the 80 percent of the subject matter that is formally needed to solve the problems is *the* core knowledge.

Building a Repertoire of Problems. In PBL, students learn to use the hypothetico-deductive approach to solve unknown problems. They may not have explicit practice in using pattern recognition (Schoenfeld and Herrmann, 1982) to solve familiar problems. Part of the dilemma in using PBL is the number of problems and sample solutions to which students are exposed compared to the conventional program (my estimate is ten problems in the conventional program for every one problem in a PBL program) and part is the degree of explicit training in pattern recognition through elaboration that is required of the student groups. Two interventions I use with students in our PBL program are to include a feedback meeting and to require students to elaborate about the new knowledge by explicitly creating a variety of problem-situations. In the feedback meeting, students pose typical exam questions for each other, representing new knowledge gained. In the elaboration activities, students are asked to create ten other problems that they could solve based on the same fundamental principles. They also elaborate by looking for similar problems, ones that have similar symptoms but different solutions.

Skill in Identifying Issues. In conventional programs, the learning issues and objectives are selected by the faculty. Thus, students see clearly 100 percent of the objectives planned in the curriculum. In PBL programs, Dolmans, Gijselaers, Schmidt, and Van der Meer (1993) have found that students, with the help of a tutor, can generate about 60 percent of the objectives planned in the curriculum. For our use of PBL in tutorless groups, students' identifying the major learning objectives is an issue. In the mid-1980s, I gave the students the objectives for each problem. The students quickly discarded the problem and focused solely on my objectives. For the past four years, I have successfully asked the students to create their own objectives, but then I validate their objectives during the goals meeting before they continue. Students can identify between 50 percent and 80 percent of the curriculum objectives by themselves.

Program Evaluation

The chemical engineering program has many components, one of which is small group, self-directed PBL as part of two required courses. To evaluate the overall program, I have used a variety of measures to assess students' acceptance of the learning environment, their marks, their confidence, their problem-solving skills, their process skills, and their attitude toward lifetime learning. I have also collected data on alumni, recruiter, and employer responses.

Learning Environment. Students' response to a course perceptions questionnaire was more positive, by one standard deviation, than that of a control group of engineering students who were not enrolled in our program.

Marks. We made a two-year study of students' marks in a chemical engineering course. Students' marks improved on written three-hour exams when they concurrently took the processing skills course compared with a control group of students taking the same chemical engineering course but without the course in processing skills. The degree improvement was statistically significant for the two years of the study.

Confidence with Problem-Solving Skills. Students' mean scores on Heppner's Problem Solving Inventory (PSI) (Heppner and Petersen, 1982) changed positively by one to two standard deviations. Students completed the inventory when they first entered the program; the same inventory was used as a post-test for the same students three or four years later (depending on whether the student was registered in a four- or five-year program). For the control group of students in engineering programs without the required courses in processing skills and PBL, PSI scores changed negligibly over the three or four years. Heppner's PSI assesses confidence in problem solving, willingness to engage in solving challenging problems, and sense of control of the problem-solving situation.

Processing Skills. In each of the three years of the program, students wrote two- or three-hour written examinations assessing their processing skills. Class average marks were 75 percent to 82 percent over the past ten years. In addition, the Billings-Moos test (Billings and Moos, 1981) showed positive improvements in scores on both avoidance and problem solving in each successive year. The Billings-Moos inventory asks one to reflect on a stressful event encountered in the past year and note the degree to which one used thirty different coping strategies. The strategies that Billings and Moos found to have a significant impact on success in coping were avoidance and problem solving.

Attitude Toward Lifetime Learning. The Perry inventory (1970) changed from an average of about 3.5 in the third year to an average of 4.6 in the final year as measured by either the Gainen or Moore-Fitch scales (Woods, 1994). The Perry inventory identifies attitude toward learning, the roles of the instructor and of the student, preferred tasks, characteristics of knowledge, and attitudes toward assessment. The closer the value is to 5, the more in tune the student's attitudes are with self-directed learning and open-ended problem solving.

In another study, we created PBL groups based on grade point so that all of the groups had approximately the same grade point average. After six weeks of PBL activity, we measured the degree to which each group was comfortable with self-directed learning. Those groups where all five members were performing as interdependent self-directed learners at the six-week mark scored an average of 9 marks higher on written three-hour examinations of subject knowledge than groups having two or fewer members functioning as interdependent self-directed learners with the others preferring more traditional ways of learning or having Perry scores below 3.5.

Self-Assessment Skills. In two studies, we compared the students' self-assessment with their overall performance in two courses and with their performance on written two- or three-hour examinations. The performance mark differs from the final examination mark because students contract for different weightings for the term work. That is, some may elect to have the term work count 40 percent with the final examination worth 60 percent. In one study ($N = 49$), the self-assessment marks were 1.3 percent lower than their marks for overall performance and were 6.3 percent higher than their marks on the final examination. In the second study ($N = 50$), the self-assessment marks were 1.9 percent lower than their marks for overall performance and were 1.6 percent lower than their marks on the final examination. With training, students can accurately self-assess, and we should empower them with that responsibility more frequently.

Alumni and Recruiter Response. In a blind survey of graduates one to five years from the program ($N = 48$), 58 percent of the alumni reported that the courses they found most important for their current professional progress and working were the processing skills and PBL courses in our curriculum, more than twice as many as those who cited the emphasis on engineering fundamentals (25 percent) or project work (10 percent). One alumnus wrote, "If you learn nothing else in chemical engineering, remember everything you learn in the PBL and problem solving courses." Another wrote, "The process skills that are developed from day one in the Chemical Engineering program . . . puts the McMaster graduate above engineers from other schools."

Employers' responses have been very positive as well. One employer formerly recruited on fifteen campuses across Canada, then on five and now on three, of which McMaster is one. Another employer praised our graduates for their ability to "think for themselves and solve problems upon graduation," whereas for employees from two other chemical engineering schools in Canada, the company had to spend a year to a year and a half training the new hires before they could think for themselves. A third employer requested that another university implement identified parts of our problem-solving program before the company would recruit from their campus. Six additional employers have hired me or graduates of our program to give in-house workshops on problem solving similar to the ones we give as required components of our program.

The alumni and employer responses are difficult to interpret because our program includes many elements. Yet employers identify the problem solving and group process skills as clearly identifiable attributes that our graduates possess.

Summary

To solve the dilemma of providing more specialized courses, developing processing skills, and improving learning, we implemented a new curriculum in 1982. Two of the elements in the new curriculum were four courses to explicitly develop processing skills and the use of small group, self-directed PBL as parts of two courses. The major issues we addressed were acceptance by the faculty and by the students, deciding how and when to develop the processing skills, working with tutorless groups, monitoring students' accountability, and maintaining the students' attention to the PBL course in an otherwise conventional program. In addition, we tried to maintain the reported strengths of PBL and at the same time to address possible weaknesses: content coverage, developing problem solving and pattern recognition approaches, and developing skills in identifying learning issues.

Over the past thirteen years, we have evaluated our program. On virtually all measures, our students show a marked superiority in the skills that are in demand in the real world—strong support for what started as only a small piece of a larger pie.

References

Albanese, M. A., and Mitchell, S. "Problem-Based Learning: A Review of Literature on Its Outcomes and Implementation Issues." *Academic Medicine,* 1993, *68* (1), 52–81.

Billings, A. G., and Moos, R. H. "The Role of Coping Responses and Social Resources in Attenuating the Stress of Life Events." *Journal of Behavioral Medicine,* 1981, *4* (2), 139–157. (Available as the Coping Responses Inventory CRI from Psychological Assessment Resources, P.O. Box 998, Odessa FL 33556.)

Bradford School of Technical Management. *Managerial Skills and Expertise Used by Samples of Engineers in Britain, Australia, Western Canada, Japan, the Netherlands and Norway.* Technical Report TMR 152. Bradford, England: University of Bradford, 1984.

Chickering, A. W., and Gamson, Z. F. "Seven Principles for Good Practice in Undergraduate Education." *AAHE Bulletin,* 1987, *3,* 3–7.

Dolmans, D.H.J.M., Gijselaers, W. H., Schmidt, H. G., and Van der Meer, S. B. "Problem Effectiveness in a Course Using Problem-Based Learning." *Academic Medicine,* 1993, *68* (3), 207–213.

Heppner, P. P., and Petersen, C. H. "The Development and Implications of a Personal Problem-Solving Inventory." *Journal of Counseling Psychology,* 1982, *291,* 66–75. (Available as Problem Solving Inventory from CPP, P.O. Box 10096, Palo Alto CA 94303–0979.)

Knapper, C. *Course Perceptions Questionnaire.* Kingston, Ontario: Instructional Development Center, Queens University, 1994.

Norman, G. A., and Schmidt, H. G. "The Psychological Basis of Problem-Based Learning: A Review of the Evidence." *Academic Medicine,* 1992, *67* (9), 557–565.

Perry, W. G., Jr. *Forms of Intellectual and Ethical Behavior in the College Years.* Austin, Tex.: Holt, Reinhart and Winston, 1970.

Ramsden, P. *The Lancaster Approaches to Studying and Course Perceptions Questionnaires: Lecturer's Handbook.* Oxford, England: Educational Methods Unit, Oxford Polytechnic, 1983.

Resnick, L. *Education and Learning to Think.* Washington, D.C.: National Academy Press, 1987.

Rush, J. C., Krmpotic, J. A., and Evers, F. T. *Making the Match.* Montreal: Corporate Higher Education Forum, 1985.

Schoenfeld, A. H., and Herrmann, D. "Problem Perception and Knowledge Structure in Expert and Novice Mathematical Problem Solvers." *Journal of Experimental Psychology: Learning, Memory and Cognition,* 1982, *8* (5), 484–494.

Sparkes, J. J. *Quality in Engineering Education.* Engineering Professor's Conference, Occasional Paper no. 1. Guilford, England: Department of Mechanical Engineering, University of Surrey, 1989.

Vernon, D.T.A., and Blake, R. L. "Does Problem-Based Learning Work? A Meta-Analysis of Evaluative Research." *Academic Medicine,* 1993, *68* (7), 550–563.

Woods, D. R. "Issues in Implementation in an Otherwise Conventional Programme." In D. J. Boud and G. Feletti (eds.), *The Challenge of Problem-Based Learning.* New York: St. Martin's Press, 1991.

Woods, D. R. "On the Learning in Problem-Based Learning." *PEDAGOGUE,* 1993, *4* (2), 2–3.

Woods, D. R. *Problem-Based Learning: How to Gain the Most from PBL.* Waterdown: D. R. Woods, 1994. (Distributed by McMaster University Bookstore, Hamilton, Ontario, Canada.)

Woods, D. R. *Problem-Based Learning: Resources to Gain the Most from PBL.* Waterdown: D. R. Woods, 1995a. (Distributed by McMaster University Bookstore, Hamilton, Ontario, Canada.)

Woods, D. R. *Problem-Based Learning: Helping Your Students Gain the Most from PBL.* Waterdown: D. R. Woods, 1995b. (Distributed by McMaster University Bookstore, Hamilton, Ontario, Canada.)

Woods, D. R., Crowe, C. M., Taylor, P. A., and Wood, P. E. "The MPS Program for Explicitly Developing Problem Solving Skill." In *1984 ASEE Conference Proceedings.* Washington, D.C.: American Society for Engineering Education, 1984.

Woods, D. R., Duncan-Hewitt, W., Hall, F., Eyles, C., and Hrymak, A. N. *Tutored Versus Tutorless Groups.* Hamilton, Ontario: Chemical Engineering Department, McMaster University, 1995.

DONALD R. WOODS *is professor of chemical engineering, McMaster University, Hamilton, Ontario, Canada.*

Although adapted for each particular course, problem-based learning is described in a remarkably consistent way by the authors in this issue.

Concluding Comments

LuAnn Wilkerson, Wim H. Gijselaers

Common to many of the stories in this issue is a complaint about the skills of university graduates. In business, education, science, architecture, and medicine, we are concerned to note that our graduates possess a knowledge base that is too theoretical and abstract, that they are out of touch with important problems of society or their discipline, and that they lack communication skills. Our authors have turned to problem-based learning (PBL) as one means of addressing these concerns. In a problem-based classroom, students are actively engaged in constructing knowledge and developing skills in using that knowledge for problem analysis and resolution through self-directed study and collaborative discussion.

Common Features Across PBL Applications

Although the details of a particular application may differ, these articles suggest that problem-based learning is characterized by at least three common features. First, PBL is student-centered. Learners play a role in determining what will be learned and in what way. They are active participants in class, asking questions, offering possible explanations, and critically appraising evidence. Prompted by the problems, they collaborate in inquiring and explaining. There is less need than in the traditional university classroom for the teacher to employ Socratic questioning or provide detail-rich lectures.

Second, teachers in problem-based courses take on different roles than they do in lecture-based courses. They are facilitators rather than disseminators; observers rather than actors. They coach from the sidelines, providing constructive feedback and challenging students to excel. They lead indirectly through the problems that they include and the questions that they ask. They

NEW DIRECTIONS FOR TEACHING AND LEARNING, no. 68, Winter 1996 © Jossey-Bass Publishers

know when to step into the students' discussion to refocus or probe for deeper understanding and when to remain quiet while students struggle to construct a correct explanation or solution.

Third, in problem-based learning, problems serve as the initial stimulus and framework for learning. They are introduced early in the process of learning new material, not after a series of lectures or assigned readings. These problems are different from the calculations or recitation questions found at the end of a textbook chapter. They are complex, ill-structured, multidisciplinary, and meaningful. They engage students in problem-solving behaviors relevant to the discipline under study. They require skills in analysis, synthesis, and evaluation. They provoke, puzzle, and surprise. Students and teacher alike care about understanding and answering them.

Wim Gijselaers reminds us in his chapter about the learning principles at work in problem-based courses. New learning requires the activation of prior knowledge and the active construction of richly elaborated relationships among ideas. These networks or schema make it possible for learners to retain new concepts and skills, and through practice during the process of learning, to organize them in a variety of ways for use in familiar and unfamiliar situations. Knowledge embedded in a context similar to that in which it may eventually be used is more easily recalled than isolated knowledge. Students' interactions provide a means of their clarifying and constructing new understanding. Finally, the ability to monitor one's own learning processes and to reflect on experience for the purpose of expanding from the specific instance to generalized understanding are skills required for a lifetime of learning.

Problem-based learning has the potential to activate these principles but may fail to do so. Common problems in the implementation of problem-based learning described by the authors in this issue include teacher behavior that is too passive, curricular structures that are too rigid, and problems that are inappropriate for the articulated goals.

The authors who describe the use of PBL in the various disciplines are remarkably consistent in their descriptions of the types of problems that are most effective. First, they suggest that the manner in which a problem is encountered by the learners is dependent on the objectives to be accomplished. For example, if one of the goals of instruction is for students to acquire skills in asking questions, problems should be constructed in such a way that students have to pose questions to obtain details of the situation. In medical education, this has been done through the use of actors standardized to portray particular patients; in educational leadership, through visits to discussion groups of a standardized student or parent. Second, problems represent high-impact situations. They are provocative, compelling, or controversial. In the McMaster inquiry course, they are selected by students based on their personal interests and everyday lives as citizens. Third, they are ill-structured, that is to say, the application of a clear set of rules will not lead to an easy explication or resolution. They are complex and messy. In calculus, the computation is merely a tool in resolving a larger issue involved in the design of a water system. Finally, they are the types of problems that practitioners of the discipline encounter on a regular basis. In engineering, they are problems of system design. In biology, they are puzzling natural phenomena. In business, they are marketing dilemmas to be resolved or new business plans to be developed. Above all, effective problems compel the learner to become involved in seeking to understand and resolve them.

Several of the authors in this volume provide suggestions for the teacher who desires to shift from a teacher-centered to a student-centered role. John Stinson and Richard Milter describe this type of change as the movement from the sage-on-the-stage to the guide-by-the-side. The problem-based teacher must be comfortable at relinquishing authority and skilled at exerting indirect control through selection of problems and the use of probing questions. He or she must become a skilled observer, able to determine when to intervene to terminate an unproductive aspect of the discussion, and when to let a mistake be followed to its illogical conclusion. The effective PBL teacher is attentive to the social and academic interactions among students and skilled in maximizing both the task and process aspects of group discussions. Finally, he or she can demonstrate problem-solving strategies predominant in the discipline without denying students the opportunity to practice using those strategies. Knowing how to say "I don't know" and acknowledging mistakes are critical skills for the role model in any discipline.

Finally, you will have noticed that problem-based learning can be used in the college classroom in a variety of ways. In the educational leadership course, the students work in teams for three to five class sessions of three hours each. The teams are entirely student managed with the leader, facilitator, and recorder roles rotated among members. In the business education curriculum, students work both individually and in groups on eight large projects, each of which includes whole-class sessions for debriefings and demonstrations. In the science courses at Delaware, problems are introduced via a minilecture to the whole class, then turned over to permanent working groups with the instructor guiding several groups simultaneously. Problems contain break points that allow the instructor to bring the small groups together for purposes of clarification or distribution of new information relevant to the problem at hand. In the calculus course at Ithaca College, in-class problem-situations are used to generate curiosity and provide students individual practice in translating everyday language into mathematical information or vice versa while larger projects are tackled by student teams both in and outside of class. Resource and space constraints are seen by these authors as opportunities for creative adaptations of problem-based learning rather than as a signal that PBL cannot be done in their particular setting.

Additional Resources

Each article contains references noted by the authors as important in their own work in problem-based learning. We recommend these as a starting point for exploring the educational theories at work in problem-based learning, for considering studies done of the process and outcomes of problem-based learning, or for learning more about strategies for implementation. Should you desire to discuss these issues or exchange cases with university teachers around the world, you might want to subscribe to the PBLIST list server on the Internet. To do so, send the command

SUBSCRIBE PBLIST Firstname Lastname

in the body of an e-mail message addressed to

listproc@sparky.uthscsa.edu

LuANN WILKERSON is associate dean for medical education and director of the Center for Educational Development and Research, University of California, Los Angeles, School of Medicine.

WIM H. GIJSELAERS is associate professor of education at the department of educational development and educational research, University of Limburg, Maastricht, the Netherlands.

INDEX

ORDERING INFORMATION

NEW DIRECTIONS FOR TEACHING AND LEARNING is a series of paperback books that presents ideas and techniques for improving college teaching, based both on the practical expertise of seasoned instructors and on the latest research findings of educational and psychological researchers. Books in the series are published quarterly in Spring, Summer, Fall, and Winter and are available for purchase by subscription as well as by single copy.

SUBSCRIPTIONS cost $52.00 for individuals (a savings of 35 percent over single-copy prices) and $79.00 for institutions, agencies, and libraries. Please do not send institutional checks for personal subscriptions. Standing orders are accepted. Prices subject to change. (For subscriptions outside of North America, add $7.00 for shipping via surface mail or $25.00 for air mail. Orders *must be prepaid* in U.S. dollars by check drawn on a U.S. bank or charged to VISA, MasterCard, or American Express.)

SINGLE COPIES cost $20.00 plus shipping (see below) when payment accompanies order. California, New Jersey, New York, and Washington, D.C., residents please include appropriate sales tax. Canadian residents add GST and any local taxes. Billed orders will be charged shipping and handling. No billed shipments to post office boxes. (Orders from outside North America *must be prepaid* in U.S. dollars by check drawn on a U.S. bank or charged to VISA, MasterCard, or American Express.)

SHIPPING (SINGLE COPIES ONLY): $10.00 and under, add $2.50; to $20.00, add $3.50; to $50.00, add $4.50; to $75.00, add $5.50; to $100.00, add $6.50; to $150.00, add $7.50; over $150.00, add $8.50.

DISCOUNTS FOR QUANTITY ORDERS are available. Please write to the address below for information.

ALL ORDERS must include either the name of an individual or an official purchase order number. Please submit your order as follows:
　　Subscriptions: specify series and year subscription is to begin
　　Single copies: include individual title code (such as TL54)

MAIL ALL ORDERS TO:
　　Jossey-Bass Publishers
　　350 Sansome Street
　　San Francisco, CA 94104-1342

FOR SUBSCRIPTION SALES OUTSIDE OF THE UNITED STATES, CONTACT:
　　any international subscription agency or Jossey-Bass directly.

OTHER TITLES AVAILABLE IN THE
NEW DIRECTIONS FOR TEACHING AND LEARNING SERIES
Robert J. Menges, Editor-in-Chief
Marilla D. Svinicki, Associate Editor